To Rich.
You are a
me.

D0863546

I'm From Division Street

by

Kenneth N. Green

authorHOUSE®

AuthorHouse™
1663 Liberty Drive, Suite 200
Bloomington, IN 47403
www.authorhouse.com
Phone: 1-800-839-8640

First published by AuthorHouse 10/1/2008

ISBN: 978-1-4343-2206-7 (sc)

Printed in the United States of America
Bloomington, Indiana

This book is printed on acid-free paper.

Division Street

Recently, I was referred to an orthopedic doctor in Beverly Hills because of problems with my back. He was Jewish, like me, and looked my age. Dr. Ted Goldstein said, "You're a tough guy. I can tell. Where are you from?" Me: "Chicago." Dr. Goldstein: "Me, too. What neighborhood?" Me: "Division Street." Goldstein looked at me, smiled, and said, "I knew you were tough." Anyone who has lived in Chicago during the 1940s, '50s, and early '60s knows that the tough guys were from Division Street. What I mean by "tough" is not necessarily physically tough. It is an attitude that states, "I will succeed no matter what."

Division Street shaped my life. Everything that I am is because of my experiences on Division Street.

When I entered high school, like all of my Jewish friends, I applied for a permit to go to Roosevelt High School, which was about ten miles away. It required two buses to get there and took an hour. I would get up at 5:45 a.m. and walk several blocks to the bus stop. Why? I wanted to go to this better school that had higher-class kids than those who went to Tuley, which was the school in my district. According to my dear friend, Earl Pick, who lived across the street from Roosevelt High School, I and all of my buddies from Division Street seemed totally out of place and inadequate. We knew that our parents had less money than the kids who lived next to Roosevelt (Albany Park). Even more important, though, was what we perceived to be our lack of culture. For my group of friends to go to the other side of town to Roosevelt was like a hillbilly from Arkansas relocating to Brooklyn. We stuck out like sore thumbs. Most of the kids were afraid of us, but we did have a mystique that attracted the girls to us. We just never felt comfortable being with the Albany Park kids. Throughout my entire adult life, I have attributed differences between myself and other people to the fact that I came from Division Street.

For example, my hideous failure in my required speech class in college, which will be mentioned later. Even though I became a well-known criminal defense attorney and adjunct professor at UCLA, and I am on a first-name basis with California Supreme Court Justices, police chiefs, and politicians, I still have a Division Street feeling of inadequacy when I am around the "North Siders" who attended my high school. I attended my fortieth high school reunion in Chicago, and when I saw my classmates from the North Side that I had not seen in forty years, my feeling of inadequacy returned. How can I explain this when I am so comfortable around other people who I have worked with, of high station?

Why were the kids from Division Street so different from the North Siders? My father and all my friends' fathers walked around their apartments in their underwear, whereas the North Siders' fathers wore slippers and robes, and many smoked pipes. Their fathers played catch with them, and ours never did. Their fathers would send them away to college, and our fathers would ask, "Vy do you want to go away, don't you like it here?" Our parents spoke Yiddish at home, while their parents couldn't speak it if they had to. Their parents took vacations with them, and our parents did not know what the word vacation meant. Our fathers were all gamblers, and their fathers were not. Our neighborhood had mixed races and religions, and their neighborhood was all Jewish. The boys on the North Side had no difficulty talking to girls and teachers. They seemed very self-assured. My boys, although we had many girlfriends, had great difficulty socializing with girls when we were young.

On my first day at Roosevelt High School, I was as scared as I was when I did my first jury trial. I thought, "What am I doing here?" All the boys were wearing cashmere sweaters and they looked like they went to prep schools, and I felt like a member of the Dead End Kids.

And perhaps what most defined the differences between the Division Street boys and the North Side boys, in my mind, was when I started high school and asked my father for money to go buy underwear and socks. He told me that I could wear his underwear and his socks, which I did all through high school, but had to use a diaper pin to hold up the shorts. I believed that all boys wore their fathers' underwear.

It was because I was from Division Street that I was awkward in speaking to my junior high and high school classes when I was a teacher. I had to speak slowly so there wouldn't be any "dees, dems, or dose." Conversely, I was advantaged as a trial lawyer and adjunct professor at UCLA because the jurors and my students were able to relate to me. Thanks to you, Division Street.

The area of Division Street where I lived is bordered by the famous Humboldt Park (named after the naturalist, Alexander von Humboldt). Those who lived on the east side of the park on Division Street and adjoining side streets were the lower class. I lived on the east side, a few blocks from the famous corner of Division and California, where the landmark restaurant The Humboldt Spot, later renamed Ricky's, was located.

The street ran east and west, as far east as Lake Michigan, where the city ended, and as far west as Harlem Avenue. The street had all kinds of shops on both the north and south side of the street, and almost all of the proprietors were Jewish.

Thousands of Eastern European Jews immigrated to Chicago around 1890, coming from Romania, Bohemia, Hungary, and Austria. The Jews originally settled in a half-mile area east of Humboldt Park. Eventually, they started to move west of the park where the buildings were newer and the apartments larger.

The Jewish people built many synagogues, or shuls, as we were taught to call them. In those days, a good Jew would never refer to a shul as a temple; God would strike us dead. Where I lived, you couldn't walk more than a few blocks without seeing a shul. The Austro-Galican (aka Galisianer) Congregation was the largest shul on the east side of the park. It was on the corner of California and Hirsch. The last rabbi was Moses Eichenstein, who continued as the rabbi even after the shul moved to a more affluent neighborhood. The famous cantor, Richard Tucker, frequently sang at this shul.

During the end of the nineteenth century, German and Scandinavian families also settled in the Humboldt Park area, and by the beginning of the twentieth century, Italians, Poles, and Eastern European Jews also moved in.

By 1940, when I was two years old, the population of Humboldt Park by Division Street was approximately 80,000 people. Most of them were Italians, Germans, Poles, and Russian Jews. By 1960, Humboldt Park was 99% white, with Italians being the largest ethnic group, followed by Poles, and German and Russian Jews. The minority were Puerto Ricans and blacks. By 1990, the inhabitants of Humboldt Park were one-third Hispanic (mostly Puerto Rican), one-third black, and one-third white.

Humboldt Park

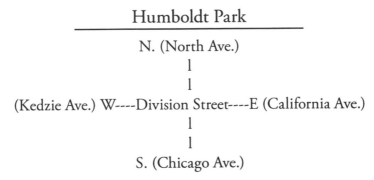

N. (North Ave.)

(Kedzie Ave.) W----Division Street----E (California Ave.)

S. (Chicago Ave.)

At the entrance to the park, on the corner of Division and California, was a statue of a coal miner, entitled "Home." He wore his headlight and carried a lunch pail, holding his little daughter's hand, while she was kissing his hand. Sadly, by the early 1950s, vandals had destroyed this beautiful statue. Another great statue in the park was of the Polish freedom fighter, Tadeusz Kosciuszko, on horseback. The Polish people revered him and celebrated his birthday every year at the park. It was a major event. Sundays were the biggest day at the park. It was the center of our social life. Elderly Jewish women would sit on the benches talking and eating *shiminitz* (Yiddish for sunflower seeds). Young boys would play softball on the grass and the girls would watch us. Humboldt Park was huge—it was like a city within a city.

One of the most beautiful areas of the park was the flower garden at the west end, guarded by two huge bronze buffalos.

There was Bunker Hill, which froze during the winter. We would bellyflop on our Commander sleds down this very steep hill onto the frozen lagoon. We would do that all day. No breaks; strong bladders. As I look back on my life, few things gave me more pleasure than zooming down Bunker Hill, free as a bird. I was suddenly transformed from a city boy surrounded by cement to a kid from Scandinavia.

The Indian Trail, aka Devil's Path, was where we would ride our bikes through these enchanted forestlike trails that were hidden from the busy city. This was our only exposure to country because all we knew were flat cement streets. I would visualize myself as a country boy during those bike rides. There was the boathouse pavilion that had billiard and ping-pong tables. You could also rent rowboats for twenty-five cents an hour at the beautiful lagoon in the park.

I have a clear memory of my family and our neighbors sleeping on blankets in the park during the unbearably hot summers. There was no air-conditioning then. We used punks (slow-burning insect repellant sticks) to ward off the mosquitoes. We did not know from crime; no one was afraid to sleep in the park.

Windy City Softball, Etc.

We would start playing when the sun came up and didn't stop until it got so dark we couldn't see the ball. You choose up sides by lobbing a bat to another guy, who would place his hand on the bat and you and he would continue hand over hand until the last hand reached the handle. That boy got to pick the first player for his team. And so it went, until two teams were selected.

Softball in Chicago is different than softball anywhere else. It's called "Windy City Ball." It's played with a sixteen-inch clincher, as opposed to the twelve-inch balls that are used in Los Angeles and elsewhere. As the game went on, the ball got softer; we wore no gloves. I loved the smell of the ball and the feel of it. Had the law allowed, I would have married a sixteen-inch clincher.

Some of the greatest athletes I ever knew played softball with me. Rojac, Zeke, Andy Buschardi. Each of them could throw you out at home plate from the outfield—on the fly. "Windy City Ball" is played with ten guys to a team. The extra man played short center field, which is between second base and centerfield. Pitching is underhand, but speed and accuracy are not sacrificed. When you were selected by the captain of the team, and you heard your name, it was as if you were elected to baseball's Hall of Fame. By the way, the captains were self-appointed. The best player would always say, "I will be the captain."

There were some kids in the neighborhood who weren't close friends, but I went to grammar school with them, and some of them also attended Tuley High School with me after I was thrown out of

Roosevelt. These were Polish guys who always hung together. There was Steve Luckashevitz (became Steve Lucas), John Jurasic, and Gabula. They were very tough kids. Luckashevitz had a huge growth spurt when he was about sixteen, and shot up to 6'3", and was a star basketball player at Tuley High School. Six foot three in those days was like seven feet today.

The neighborhood had a lot of schools. The grammar schools were Von Humboldt (my school), Schley, Lowell, and La Fayette. The high school was Tuley. However, most of the Jewish kids obtained transfers to go to Roosevelt High, which was in Albany Park.

My closest friends were Dino, the Shlub, Mitch "Coo" Cohen, Gerry Zaidman, Jerry Starkman, and Johnny Walker. Also on my block were Angie, Salvatore, Ears, Genue, and Stash, whom I got along with, but we weren't tight. The strange names will be explained later.

In my neighborhood, you were guaranteed a serious beating if you brought books home from school or wore short pants in the summer. I followed those rules carefully and was thrown out of high school. I had never, ever, read a book until I entered college. Yet, I became a high school teacher, then a highly regarded criminal defense attorney in Los Angeles. I worked my way up to Bureau Chief of the Los Angeles County Public Defender's Office, where I supervised 360 attorneys plus 150 support staff. For a kid who got thrown out of high school, I didn't do so badly. My high school vice principal, George Okerbey, would turn over in his grave if he knew of my success. The deputy district attorney who was assigned to the Robert Blake case had been my opponent in several jury trials. His name is Pat Dixon. Whenever I run into him at a legal affair, he tells people that I used to beat him regularly and that I am an outstanding lawyer. Additionally, I was recently called for jury duty. It was to be a protracted trial and there were seven lawyers on the case. When I was called to sit in "the box," I had to answer questions on the blackboard: my name, my occupation (I answered, "Attorney"), whether I was single or married, and my wife's occupation (I answered, "Deputy District Attorney"). The judge then told the litigants and their attorneys and the jury that he knew me for over thirty years and that we used to try cases against each other when he was a prosecutor. He went on to say that I used to beat the pants off of him regularly and that I was an outstanding trial lawyer and a chief administrator of the public defender's office. My parents would have *kvelled* (Yiddish for jump for joy).

I have also been an adjunct professor at UCLA for the past twenty-seven years, where I teach criminal law to paralegals. Additionally, I realized my boyhood dream of boxing with, and becoming friends with, many world champion boxers.

My Teachers' Predictions
How Wrong They Were

I was supposed to end up at Joliet Prison or, at best, working at the corner gas station. This, according to my teachers.

A few years ago, my sister was purchasing lipstick at the cosmetic counter at Robinson's-May Department Store in Los Angeles. My sister told the saleslady that she detected a Chicago accent. Sister: "Are you from Chicago?" Saleslady: "Yes, but I'm older than you." Sister: "I have a brother who is a lawyer named Kenny Green, who is about your age, do you know him?" Saleslady: "I knew a Kenny Green, but he would definitely not be a lawyer; he would be dead from the electric chair." My sister got her phone number and I called and chatted with her. She was my old friend, Lenore Munder.

I return to Division Street every year. I began doing this ten years ago. I rent a car and I drive to an area that holds a strong memory; for example, the storefront that housed my father's paint shop (where he kept his ladders and paint) or my bubbie's fruit and vegetable store that used to have sawdust on the floor. I turn off the engine and visualize myself as a young boy being there. I should add that my wife and I always stay at the famous Ambassador East Hotel, where presidents and celebrities used to stay when I was a boy. The famous Pump Room restaurant at the hotel has their photographs on all the walls, and my wife and I sit in the booths that these famous people sat in. As a boy, this would have been beyond my wildest dreams.

I also hit (a Chicago expression meaning to "visit") every hot dog stand and Italian beef sandwich shop in the city. And my cholesterol climbs to world-class levels. (My wife, Maureen, insisted that I define "hit" even though I insisted it wasn't necessary.)

7

Over the years, I had heard about famous people, mostly Jewish, who had lived on Division Street just blocks from where I lived. My list keeps growing: Benny Goodman (famous bandleader), Barney Ross (welterweight boxing champion of the world), Studs Turkel (Pulitzer Prize-winning author), Saul Bellow (Pulitzer Prize-winning author), Sherman Block (owned the tiny Itzcovitz Deli on Division Street before becoming not only Sheriff of Los Angeles County, but one of the most powerful politicians in the state), Ben Hecht (famous movie director), Doctor G. G. Molinari (world famous biologist), Julius Echeles (famous attorney), Art Petacque (Pulitzer Prize-winning crime reporter, who was the brother of legendary cop Lieutenant Dave Petacque), Michael Todd (movie producer, married to Elizabeth Taylor), Rosalyn Turk (concert pianist), Isaac Rosenfeld (famous author), Jackie Leonard (aka Fats Levinsky, famous comedian), Carl Foreman (famous Hollywood producer), Mickey Rotner (Jewish Basketball Hall of Fame), Doctor Jules Stein (established the Jules Stein Eye Clinic at UCLA), Baby Face Nelson (infamous gangster), Alderman Tom Keene (Mayor Daley's right-hand man, who played a major role in John Kennedy's election to president), Jerry Blumenthal (a classmate who produced the movie *White Men Can't Jump*), and many more.

After I discovered that so many famous people came from this impoverished neighborhood, I decided that I must find out what there was about them and this neighborhood that made them rise to such prominence. There must be something magical about Division Street, I believed. We were all poor, but we didn't know it. We had a toughness and drive that was unstoppable.

We did not use drugs or alcohol. We were just tough guys determined to succeed in life. We loved girls, cars, and sports, in that order.

Division Street Landmarks and Institutions and Characters

The most famous of all the establishments on Division Street was Nate's Barbershop, just east of California Avenue on the north side of the street. The legendary Nate Levine was the owner. I called him uncle because he was so close to my parents. My mother was his manicurist.

It was at his shop that my father met my mother, in 1935. There were three barber chairs, a manicure table, and a shoeshine stand. On the walls of the shop were posters for Wildroot Cream Oil and Vitalis and Brylcream, which slicked back your hair. I can still smell these lotions.

All the politicians of the Thirty-First Ward under Alderman Tom Keene, as well as all the cops in the neighborhood and a number of gangsters, hung out there and played cards in the back room (off duty, the cops and hoods got along). Nate was right out of Damon Runyon; a dees, dems, and dose guy who never learned to read or write, but was appointed chief bailiff of Cook County, through patronage. If anyone got a traffic ticket, they paid Nate, direct!

My barber was Bennie the Bookie. He was slim and nervous. He parted his hair down the middle. Poor Bennie couldn't get through a haircut without taking at least six bets on the phone, but Bennie was a great man—he could have been a surgeon, he had really great hands. While he was cutting my hair, he'd whisper, "Don't move—stay still."

The Humboldt Spot, later renamed Ricky's, was the deli located on the corner of Division and California. Everybody hung out there. Corned beef sandwiches were fifty cents, including cole slaw and pickles. Art Melmen owned it. Today, his son Ricky is one of the biggest restaurateurs in the country.

One of the higher class restaurants on Division Street, a quarter block east, was named Stelzer's, which had a canopy. This was the only restaurant that changed tablecloths daily.

Joe Pierce Deli, which was two blocks east of Ricky's, was the workingman's deli. They served the best hot corned beef in Chicago. The famous chocolate phosphate was created here by counterman Hyman Weiss. He mixed chocolate syrup with seltzer water and it became the most popular soft drink in Chicago. Speaking of corned beef, it had the most mouth-watering smell. To a Jew, corned beef is the elixir of life.

Brown and Kopple was another deli that had once been the hangout for Al Capone. It was on Division and Damon.

Jack Weber's Parklane Pool Hall was where my father and most of my friends' fathers spent a good portion of their lives playing cards: poker and pinochle for money. Weber got a house "cut" of the action. It was illegal to play for money, and I recall many occasions being with my father during one of those card games, when the owner, Jack Weber, would get a warning call that the police were on the way to raid them. Guess who the caller was? You guessed! One of the other police stations that was on Weber's payroll.

Speaking of police corruption, everyone knew the expression "captain's man." This was the bagman for the police captain. Every police captain was on the take. But they had deniability by providing a buffer between them and the briber.

The Chicago Police Department was not politically correct when I was growing up. What they used to do when they caught a suspected burglar was to take him down to the basement of the police station and just keep beating on him. In fact, they would start beating him with their nightsticks in the car. One particular case that I remember very well was when my father, who was a painting contractor, had several guys working for him at one time. Several of them were from the south, and we referred to them as "hillbillies." One of them was named Jarvis. He was quiet, but mean. Jarvis decided that he had a grievance with my father, and in order to punish my father, he was going to steal his ladders. My father was unable to do any other work without these extension ladders. So my father called up his good friend, Detective Jack Lerner, and without going through channels, Lerner said, "I'll take care of it." Lerner, his partner Larry, my father, and I drove to Jarvis's apartment in an unmarked police car; Lerner and Larry told my father and me to wait at the foot of the stairs. Lerner and Larry walked up the winding staircase with their snub nose .38s out, and yelled, "Jarvis, come on out, it's the Chicago Police Department." Jarvis came out and turned over the ladders, and that was the end of it. My father bought Lerner a bottle of Seagram's, and that's how the Chicago Police Department worked: instant justice.

During WWII, Jewish men from all over the northwest side would meet at Weber's pool hall. Whenever there was a German Bund meeting in the neighborhood, ten "Lantzmen" would pile into each car holding poolsticks out the windows, which were used to beat the Nazis at their meeting.

George the Greek had a horse-drawn wagon and a monkey. The wagon was painted red with yellow trim and shiny brass ornaments. The upper half was glass with sliding windows. He sold waffles and flavored ice, either one for five cents. George never used the reins on the horse. The horse knew exactly where to go and when to stop.

Every alley had peddlers riding through with a horse and buggy. Some sold "water-melone." (This is how the peddler pronounced watermelon when he called out to the people.) Also, there were peddlers buying rags and iron, and they would call out "Rags, Old Iron." For years, I thought they said, "Rags a Line."

Peskins Fruit and Vegetable Stand

Jerry Peskin was my schoolmate and lived across the street from me. His father owned a fruit and vegetable stand on Division Street, and in the back, Jerry set up a fruit basket to be used as a basketball hoop. We used to shoot baskets over the watermelons. His cousin, Syd Peskin, who worked there, became a prominent orthodontist. Jerry became a famous photographer.

"The Shvitz"

Short for shvitzbah (*shvitz* in Yiddish means to sweat). This was a bathhouse. It had Turkish and Russian steam baths. My father used to take me there when I was little.

On Sundays, the men would sit in a room filled with steam and periodically throw a bucket of cold water on the rocks to generate more steam. This was a Jewish ritual. They lathered themselves up with buckets of soap applied to the body with grape leaves. None of the men were in shape. They didn't know from working out. Every one of them was extremely hairy.

After the steams, the men would wrap a big white towel around themselves and go into the small room that served snacks and sandwiches. They would eat pickled herring with onions, anchovies, sardines, and rye bread, and they drank schnapps.

The Oak Street Beach was by the Gold Coast (a swanky area near Lake Michigan.) This was the most popular beach for the neighborhood kids. One five-cent streetcar ride got us there. And to us, Lake Michigan was the ocean; it was so big.

There were four movie theatres on Division Street: the Vision, the Harmony, the Strand, and the Biltmore. Admission was fourteen to seventeen cents. Each theatre smelled from a vermin spray. On more than one occasion, I saw a rat run down the aisle. Holloway bars (chocolate-flavored bars) were five cents, as was the popcorn. We went every Saturday. There were always two full-length movies, twenty-one cartoons, and two serials, such as Flash Gordon or Hopalong Cassidy. My favorite movies were *Frankenstein*, *Wolfman*, *Dracula*, *The Mummy*, and Army and cowboy movies with John Wayne. I have vivid memories of running through the dark alleys to get home after watching *Frankenstein* and having no doubt the monster would overtake me before I made it home. The monster, while slow, knew how to cut off the ring. Cutting off the ring is what a fighter does when his opponent is running. You point your left toe towards him and advance. It was my strong personal opinion that in a fight to the death, Frankenstein would easily beat both the Mummy and the Wolf Man.

Woolworth's Five and Dime—nothing over ten cents. God knows what we bought there for ten cents, but we felt compelled to spend a nickel because we knew we were saving money.

Down the street, heading east, was P.D. Kahn's Butter and Egg store. And a few blocks farther was Gratch Mandel Funeral Home. Nearby was Babbitt's Auto Parts, where they always had the latest in car accessories including plaid seatcovers and plastic wind wings.

Across the street was The Greek ice cream parlor. These were the days before political correctness, and every ice cream parlor was known as "The Greek" because Greek people, in fact, owned them. All of the Greek ice cream parlors were immaculate. There were red booths with white tables. Malts were twenty-five cents; milkshakes were twenty cents.

There were shoe repair shops every few blocks. The owners were always Italian. The butcher shops in the neighborhood were owned by either Jews or Poles, and the neighborhood bakeries were all Jewish.

A few blocks further east was Deborah Boys Club. This was a city-subsidized gym for kids. It had a boxing ring with heavy bags, speed bags, a basketball court, and a pool table. At age twelve, my then-best friend Sherwin Chasen and I were selected to fight three rounds in the ring in front of the whole neighborhood. His mother begged me not to hurt him because I was much stronger and always beat him when we fought. So I never threw a punch. Sherwin got the decision. I felt like a chump at the time, but now it brings back fond memories.

Nearby was Gribin's Jewelers. My grandmother use to have her old Gruen and Bulova watches serviced there.

Rosen's Bakery—a few doors away—the best bagels in Chicago, hot and fresh. The poor would get free bagels from Mr. Rosen.

Hot dog stands. You couldn't walk one mile in any direction without hitting a hot dog stand. Taverns were located every half-mile. In my neighborhood, we had Sammy's Red Hots, Freddy's Hot Dogs, and Moishe Pippick's (Yiddish for belly button) Hot Dogs. A Vienna hot dog (eight to a pound) with soft fresh poppy seed buns and French fries was twenty-five cents. If anyone ordered a hot dog with anything beside mustard, onions, and pickles, they were deemed sacrilegious and would be quickly punished by the Jewish God. A grape soda was ten cents. My pal Dino would eat twenty hot dogs in one sitting without blinking an eye. He called them "just a pill."

Pharmacies. There was "Karzens," "Lipschultz," and "Byalek's," where our parents would get their prescriptions filled. All the elderly Jewish pharmacists looked alike, glasses and partly balding. They had enormous respect from their customers, who considered them highly educated and learned. Many times, they acted as doctors for the poor. All of the pharmacies smelled of liniment, and most of the pharmacies also had soda fountains.

There were a lot of neighborhood candy stores that really lent a flavor to the neighborhood. One was called Smitty's, across the street from Von Humboldt grammar school. Virtually every kid who attended that grammar school would go to Smitty's during the lunch hour. He would sell hot dog sandwiches for thirteen cents. And he would also sell every kind of candy, like penny candies. In those days, we had what they called buttons. It was a long sheet of white paper, and it would have little candies glued to it. He would sell gumballs (five for a penny) and Halloway sticks (little chocolate bars) for five cents. What I remember about his store is that he always used the expression "pay up, kids, pay up." There were so many kids going up and down the aisles that a lot of them were stealing the candy; they were just putting it in their pockets. Poor Smitty was getting ripped off left and right. I think I was the only one who never stole from him. I just couldn't do it. I wouldn't have been able to sleep at night. I never stole anything from Smitty. I used to eat in the cafeteria every day, except Fridays, because they served fish, and I hated fish. So on Fridays, my mother would give me about fifty cents, and I would get three thirteen-cent hot dogs and a bottle of soda, and I would sit on the concrete steps right next to Smitty's store and eat there.

There was another candy store that was known by everyone who lived on or near Division Street, and that was called Mandel's. Two brothers owned that store: Izzy (for Izadore) and Charlie. Charlie was a great and vicious street fighter. He would have many fights with unruly people in the store. He would always beat them to a pulp. The Mandels were really nice guys and they liked the kids. In that store they had a number of pinball machines, and a big soda fountain, where they served chocolate phosphates and cherry cokes. They also were a currency exchange. In Chicago, a currency exchange performs the function of cashing checks for people on payday for a fee, and also advancing money for people for exorbitant interest. They would also handle motor vehicle transactions; you could renew your license plates there. Mandel's was like a jack-of-all-trades. Their chief employee was someone who we called Steve. Everyone knew that Steve was a woman, but you would never say that to Steve's face. She looked and dressed and acted like a man. She had short hair, big shoulders, and a deep voice. Steve ran the store. Mandel's was around from the time I was an infant until I was about twenty-six. It finally went out of business when Izzy died in his eighties. Mandel's was one of Chicago's legendary establishments.

There was another candy store called Lapufsky's. My elderly Aunt Esther and my Uncle Abe owned this store, and it was directly across the street from the cottage where I was born. Their son, Henry, became an engineer and then an attorney. I thought cousin Henry was a genius.

Pete's Polish delicatessen and candy store was about fifty yards from my apartment. Pete had the best ham in the world. While most of my friends would stop the Good Humor truck for ice cream, I would go to Pete's and get twenty cents' worth of either baked ham or summer sausage, a pickle, and Evervess seltzer water.

Swimming with the Fishes

As a teenager, my favorite Italian restaurant was Luigi's. The sign outside the restaurant stated "One Hundred Yards of Spaghetti." The owners were Al and his beautiful wife Connie. It was on North Avenue just blocks from where I lived.

Al was always hitting on the women customers. He looked like Al Pacino. He wore beautiful silk suits. No one cooked better pasta or pizza then Al. I still miss the pizza. Young as I was, I knew that he was involved with "the Boys." One day, my mother brought home the *Chicago Sun Times* with an article about a man who was found in the trunk of his car in the Chicago River. It was a mob hit; it was Al.

Speaking of gangsters, I was about fifteen years old when I drove with my father to the affluent suburb of River Forest, which was a very exclusive area with expensive Tudor estates. It was the home of Tony Acardo, aka "Big Tuna." He was the head of the Chicago syndicate and was arguably more powerful than Sam Giancana. My father told me to wait in the car, as he was to give an estimate to paint the house. When he returned about an hour later, he was white as a sheet. He told me that when he knocked on the door and was let in, men surrounded him with guns pointed at him. When Big Tuna came into the room, the hoods said, "This guy's a G man." Big Tuna laughed and said, "He is not a G man, he's the fucking painter." My father got the job, and for the rest of his life, he enjoyed telling people this story.

Harry Brown was an alias for Harry Dukat. If you wanted something done in the city, you called Harry. He was a commission-connected "wise guy." Growing up, I knew his son Mervyn very well. I often wondered why his father had the name Harry Brown. I thought it even more suspicious when one day, as he parked his car and headed toward his apartment, he was shot at by a bunch of men in a passing car. It wasn't until I was fifty and read a story about Chicago gangsters that I discovered that Harry Brown was in fact one of the most feared and powerful Jewish gangsters in Chicago and was a very close friend of Lucky Luciano and Al Capone.

Speaking of on the edge, my father's brother Mitchell also had larceny in him. He's now dead. He was younger than my father by

15

two years. He was always in trouble with the law. He would constantly come up with some scheme by which he was defrauding people. After his wife died, he would go out with women whom he would refer to as *shkoppis*; that's a Yiddish term for a woman who is old and used up. He would find these women who were widows; most of them were very unattractive, and they were lonely. He would romance them and steal their money. Eventually he got caught. Some of them turned him into the district attorney. He ended up having a jury trial. The famous criminal defense attorney, Jerry Geisler, who died many years ago, represented him. They called him the "attorney for the stars." The case ended with a hung jury, and the district attorney didn't refile. Mitchell got lucky; he was the father of all con men.

Growing Up

My earliest memories were the WWII years. I was three years old when Pearl Harbor was bombed. I remember that most of the single men in my neighborhood were drafted or enlisted. I remember air raid sirens going off at night, and everyone had to turn off the lights. This was very scary for little kids. Everyone listened to President Roosevelt's fireside chats. The Jewish people in my neighborhood adored Roosevelt. I remember the day he died. Everyone was crying; I was seven. Married men with children, like my father, were exempt from the draft.

My friends were Jews, Poles, and Italians. There were only two black boys at my grammar school (in those days, they were called colored people). The two boys were Thomas Douse and Luke Evans. Luke always sang "Shoo Fly Pie and Apple Pan Dowdy makes my eyes light up and my stomach say howdy."

While most of the time, we all got along, every now and then, a Christian boy would remind the Jews that we were Christ killers. This made me very angry because, to my knowledge, I had killed no one. So, I had no choice but to learn how to fight. There were no living Jewish boys from Division Street who could not fight.

Only a few of my friends were religious, although most were extremely proud to be Jewish, and would fight to the death at the sound of "dirty Jew," "sheenie," or "kike."

No one looked more Irish than my friend Mitch Cohen. With his blonde hair and blue eyes, he could have passed for Sean O'Reilly.

On Fridays, teachers used to excuse all Catholics from class early, if they said they were going to attend Catechism. Mitch Cohen became Mike Cohan. He was excused. On Yom Kippur, he reverted to Cohen. One day, several nuns went to his apartment looking for him because he didn't show up at Catechism. His mother made him pay! No movies for a month. She also chased the nuns down the stairs with a broom. She did that because she was raised in a Jewish ghetto in Russia, where Jews were beaten by Gentiles.

Leonard Feigenbaum was one of my friends who lived across the street from me. On Saturdays (*shabbus*), he had to stay indoors with the shades drawn and the lights turned off and he had to pray. It was so dark. I remember knocking on his door and inviting him to play softball but he said that God would punish him if he played on the Sabbath. Me: "God is a nice guy, and he wouldn't do that to you, Leonard; let's go play ball." A few of my other neighbors, Avrum and Label, also stayed in on *shabbus*.

My friend Al Scher's father used to "lay tsifilum." He would wrap what looked like a black strap around his arm that had a square box on his wrist and a box on his forehead. He also davened (bowed while praying). These types of religious cult-like experiences scared me. My parents were not at all religious, but if my father caught me eating pork or mixing milkets and fleischeks (dairy and meat), he would tell me this was a sin.

On the Jewish holidays, we would all go to the shul out of respect. My father and his friends would enter through the front door, and within ten minutes they were out the back door headed for the racetrack.

All of my friends were bar mitzvahed, except for me. This was a *shande* (shame). I refused to study at Hebrew school and Rabbi Lang threw me out. Once again, I expressed my disdain for academia.

Bill Shlifka was the bully in my grammar school. He had red hair. He wore his collar up. Everybody was afraid of him. He used to mess with me. One day we were at an assembly watching a program, and he was sitting next to me, and he kept messing with me, giving me the elbow, and I called him a son of a bitch. He said, "You called my mother a dog?" I didn't even know what he was talking about. He wouldn't stop.

He said I had to pay. Finally, I got so fed up, I said, "OK, I want to fight you. Follow me home, no one will break it up, I have a basement in my apartment building, we'll fight." He followed me home, and I beat him. He had no chance. I beat him easy. Like a typical bully, he never bothered me again.

My father was a wonderful man, but unfortunately, he was a compulsive gambler. I believed that every father was. I learned to read a scratch sheet (racing form) before I read "Dick and Jane."

My father played a monumental role in my life. I am what I am today because of my father. Because I had no interest in school, I was thrown out of high school. I had convinced myself that I was going to have a life of mediocrity. I would be a house painter like my father and come home each day with paint on my face and the smell of benzene in my lungs. But my father would have no part of that. He would constantly tell me how one day I would be an attorney and have a big fancy office, and my relatives would have to wait for me in the outer office because I was so busy. My relatives, of course, told my father that I would not amount to very much. Although they loved me, they were convinced that I didn't have what it takes to achieve great things. I remember numerous conversations with my father over the dining room table where he would tell me how important it was to go to college, even though he had never even graduated from grammar school. He told me, "It's better to make a living with a pencil, than with your back." Although he couldn't give me a dime, it was my father who motivated me.

My mother completed only two years of high school, and she never imagined that I would go to college. She was thrilled that I did and was extremely proud of me. She was always telling her friends about my achievements and how first I became a schoolteacher, then an attorney. My mother had a huge heart and was very warm and friendly. Everyone loved her.

My sister, Sandy, was a sweet little girl, and I always looked out for her. My Aunt Pearl (my mother's sister) was like my second mother and she always took me to museums and zoos.

From kindergarten through high school, I lived in the Ram apartment buildings. Our rent was $75 per month. There were twenty apartments and everyone in this building was a Jew except for a girl named June and her parents. The building, of course, was brick. All the apartment buildings were brick. Each apartment had radiators that were fueled by coal to keep us warm in the winter. Few apartments had two bathrooms, known as "double plumbing."

The backyard was cement and our back doors led to wooden porches with clothes lines leading from one end of the building to another. Clothespins held our clothes on the line. There were two washbasins in the basement to do laundry and a hand wringer for the wet clothes.

At one end of the building was a wooden shed. We always wondered what was in it except for rats, and they were huge and ugly. Whenever it rained, they would come out, and I used to set a trap for them with trails of cheese leading out to the middle of the yard. I owned a Daisy BB pump gun, now a collector's item, and I was a dead eye. From my porch, about thirty yards away, I probably hold the world's record for killing huge ugly rats.

Across the alley lived many Polish people, such as Genue and Stashue, and my buddy, Ronnie Kuta. Ronnie and I were always playing war games with toy guns. On the other end were the Italian families with Salvatore, Angie, Augustino, and Benedict.

My Mother's Singing.

My mother was a very sweet woman. She would have taken a bullet for me, but we did have our problems, one of which was her singing. My mother had a fairly good voice, I guess. It was very high, she was a soprano, and she admired Jeanette McDonald and Katherine Grayson. My mother at every opportunity would sing, and I would get embarrassed because I was a little boy. If we were with a group of people, she'd start to hum, and then when someone would say, "Oh, you have a nice voice," she'd say, "Oh really?" and then she'd start to sing all-out. I wanted to crawl into the Earth. It was the most painful thing for me. She also would sing at my assemblies at my grammar school at Von Humboldt. One day in particular she volunteered to sing the national anthem. She was the only parent who was up there performing. My friends were all making fun of me. I got down as low as I could in my chair. If I had had the means to cause my own death, there's no doubt in my mind I would have done it on the spot.

We all came from loving homes—even those of us who came from single-parent homes. There was not one of my friends' mothers or fathers who would not take a bullet for their kids and vice versa. That's the way it was. No analysis, no Doctor Spock.

When I was growing up, the Democratic Party paid all the poor people two dollars to vote Democratic. It was their standard practice to knock on the doors in the poor neighborhoods and give everybody two dollars on Election Day. "Good morning, Mrs. Cohen. Please remember to vote Democratic." On more than one occasion, I heard a neighbor say, "Give me four dollars and I'll vote twice."

I met Milton Berle at a roast a few years before his death. Me: "Mr. Berle, I'm a nice Jewish boy from Chicago, can I take a picture with you?" About six tough-looking Jews who obviously had a lot of affection for him surrounded Miltie. One of them said, "Where in Chicago?" Me: "Division Street." Five of the guys were from Division Street. I got the picture.

Mothers did not work outside the home. That was unheard of, except for Zaidman's and Starkman's mothers. Mrs. Zaidman worked as a seamstress for a furrier and raised Gerry and his sister Bobbi alone after her husband walked out on all of them when the kids were little. This was unheard of then. Zaidman's mother was an angel. She told her kids, "You will go to college," and she helped put them through. Mrs. Starkman (another angel) worked at a factory and gave her son Jerry all she could from her meager earnings.

Most of the fathers of my friends were lower middle class financially. But educationally and culturally they were lower class by the then-prevailing definition. They took no vacations, never attended a play or an opera, and wouldn't know a tennis racquet from a ping-pong paddle.

Not one of my friends' fathers graduated from high school. Most didn't finish grammar school. They were immigrants from the old country, but they were all world-class fathers who loved their kids.

My father, Mulya Grynblatt, didn't speak English until he was eighteen. He arrived at Ellis Island from the Polish ghetto of Bialistok along with his mother and three siblings. Preceding him by several years was his father and the other six siblings. His father died of pneumonia shortly after arriving in this country. Many of my relatives stayed in

Poland and were killed at Auschwitz by Hitler. It was fortuitous that my father's family left in 1930. Had they not, I would not be writing this book.

Although my father was one of nine children, only he and his brother Mitchell remained in Chicago. The other seven children and my grandmother all moved to Los Angeles, when I was five years old. Four of the children opened up a bakery on Wilshire Boulevard. It was a family-type bakery, and they were just making a living. One day, one of the partners, my uncle, was making the coffee cake that they were selling to their local customers, and he made a mistake in the recipe. The cake flattened out. He chopped it up into pieces and put it out on plates to give it away free. Everyone who came in and tasted it said they loved it. He tried and tried to replicate the mistake, and finally found out what it was he did wrong. They started producing it in mass quantities. They were selling it like crazy, and finally they opened up a factory and started selling for the markets. It was called Baker Boy Vienna Coffee Cake. They all became very rich, except for my father and his brother, Mitchell.

My father became a house painter. That is what many of the immigrants did. Or they became scrap iron dealers. They *shlepped izon"* (Yiddish for carried iron).

I remember when I was in the seventh grade and our teacher had each student stand up and tell the class what our fathers did for a living. Rarely did mothers work outside the home. Donny Solomon (Dino) stood tall and in a loud, clear, and proud voice said, "My father is an M.D." Teacher: "And what kind of doctor is he, Donald?" Dino: "Teacher, he is a metal dealer."

Most of our parents spoke broken English outside the house and Yiddish inside the house.

I was exposed to anti-Semitism very young and very frequently. I was in our huge cement backyard of the twenty-unit apartment building talking with some other neighbor kids, all of whom were Jewish. One of them asked me if I was going to go to college, one day. Me: "Sure." He: "Which one?" Me: "The University of Chicago." Everyone laughed. Me: "Why are you laughing?" He: "You are a Jew. Don't you know there is a quota for Jews at the University of Chicago?" I was stunned. I was about twelve years old. These kinds of experiences leave life-long scars on children. You either get very tough or you start to wring your hands. I got very tough because I refused to wring my hands.

Growing up, I heard the words "dirty Jew" more times than I can count. We had to be very tough to survive. Art Petacque, the famous Pulitzer Prize-winning author who came from Division Street, has been quoted as saying, "There was a lot of anti-Semitism in our neighborhood. Often times my friends and I would cut through Humboldt Park to go to the movies. Six or seven Gentile kids would gang up on us and take our money. I recall when non-Jews would band together and think it was great sport to go to the Spaulding Avenue Shul on the high holidays and pull the old Jews' beards. A bunch of us would wait for them and beat the hell out of them."

When I lived at the Ram apartments, my Uncle Hymie lived in the same building. He worked at a coal mine. He had a small interest in it. He drove a 1948 Packard that looked like a tank. It was black, and he never washed it once since the day he bought it. It was always parked in front of the shul. The front bumper was exactly even with the entrance to the shul. He was very nice to me. At Hanukkah, he'd give me a silver dollar. It was a lot of money in those days. He had a favorite expression; he would call me "cousin" (even though he was my uncle, he would call me "cousin"), "Cousin, you know I don't bullshit." That expression became so popular that my friend Johnny Walker started using it. Johnny would always call me cousin and tell me he doesn't bullshit. My Uncle Hymie was a real character. He looked exactly like the old-time actor, Leon Earl. He was the only Republican Jew that I knew. Everyone thought that he became a Republican only because he had money, but I liked him a lot. His wife Bashkie was committed to a mental institution at about age fifty. She had been a huge, robust woman who suddenly became very gaunt and strange looking. After she was committed, Uncle Hymie used to bring women home a few times a week and after they obviously had sex together, he'd bring them out on the porch and introduce me to them.

Genue was my next-door neighbor. His English name was Eugene. He was Polish. He was a short, stocky kid, and his haircut looked like the barber had put a bowl around his head and shaved around the bowl. I knew that his parents didn't like me. I saw it in their eyes. One day his father came home from work at the factory. He was upset with me over an argument that I had with Genue over a softball game. He called me dirty Jew and he slapped me. I also remember coming home from school crying when some Christian boys accused me of killing Jesus. I was maybe six years old, and I told my mother that I didn't understand why I was being accused of killing Jesus when I didn't even know who he was.

My mother had no fear. She and I were on a train in 1948 (I was ten). There was a big man on the train who was extolling the virtues of Hitler. My mother, without saying a word, walked up to him and spit right in his face. I loved it.

We were required, in grammar school, to stand and sing songs about Jesus especially during Christmas. I would stand, but I would not sing. I felt the tension from my Christian teachers and fellow students.

I saw some brutal fights in Chicago. One night I was with Mitch, Dino, and Starkman at Ricky's having a corned beef sandwich. It was late at night and some tough guys walked in, three of them; they looked like trouble. They were about our age, sixteen. So they sat down near us in a booth, and a couple booths over was another group of tough guys; I think there were four of them. For some reason, they were mad-dogging each other and taunting each other, and we all walked out around the same time. The two groups fought, and one of the guys kept banging his rival's head on the cement, until he lay still; I think he killed him.

One of my friends in the apartment building I lived in was "Ears," aka Billy Weinstein. Gary Feldman (who would become a doctor) and I (God forgive us) made fun of Billy's big floppy ears. We were all around twelve years old and we always would tease Ears by asking him if he could fly.

There was a downside, however. His sister, "Big Debbie," would come galloping down the back porch whenever we teased Ears, and she would take my head and pound it on the cement floor in the backyard. I still get headaches, and I still have nightmares about Big Debbie.

The men in my neighborhood were all Runyonesque. The men were "dees, dems, and dose" guys. Everyone spoke like the first Mayor Daly. They were bottom-line guys who saved the words. If you could say it in three words, why waste a sentence?

You would want any one of them in your foxhole. They were real men, not touchy feely. They would never say, "How do you really feel about this?" Each of them was a hero: a man's man.

The fathers in the building were cab drivers, house painters, factory workers, or scrap metal dealers. The kids thought this was what everyone's father did.

Another neighbor of mine was Harry Shaefer. He had three daughters, Leah, Sandra, and Sherry. Poor Sherry died when she was sixteen; it was the most horrible tragedy that occurred in our neighborhood. She had an incurable disease. Harry was a very difficult guy, a cab driver. He had been in the Navy during WWII, and he used to be very hard on me and my friend Gary Feldman. One day Gary's uncle was visiting, a real tough guy, and he told Harry he was going to kick his ass for being mean to Gary and me. From that day on, Harry never bothered us again.

On the other side of the apartment building was an old couple, Mr. and Mrs. Schecter. They had no children, and frequently when I was playing out in the back yard, we would hear Mrs. Schecter screaming while her husband was beating her. The cops would come and take him away. He was a drunk.

There was Mr. and Mrs. Kimmel. They also had no children. They were elderly people who lived on the first floor. I lived on the third floor. I used to run down the wooden back steps to go play ball. I couldn't wait to play, and Mrs. Kimmel would always yell at me for making too much noise running down the steps. My parents just told me to ignore her because she was nuts and mean.

Our apartment was always immaculate. My mother was proud to say that you could eat off of her floors. My mother insisted that anyone entering our apartment take off their shoes so they would not soil the white carpeting. Our living room furniture was covered in plastic, but it didn't matter, because no one was allowed in the living room; it was a shrine. My little sister Sandy would always go to Pete's Candy Store for me to buy me seltzer water (carbonated water) for two cents. My nickname in the neighborhood was "the Sheltzer Kid." That's how I used to pronounce it. I would ask my sister which she would rather have: a big nickel or a small dime, and she always took the nickel. My sister Sandy now lives in Las Vegas and she and her husband Herb are retired.

We had a milkman who would deliver fresh milk and eggs. We had an iceman who would bring huge blocks of ice to our apartment for our freezer, holding it with tongs over his back.

We used to play in my alley when I lived in the Ram apartments. The alley was our playground. We'd play softball. I'd also have my BB gun, and we'd shoot tin cans. Teddy the drunk used to walk through the alley and we all made fun of him. We were kids and we didn't know any better. We'd yell, "There's Teddy, the drunk," and he'd try to catch us but he could barely walk. And that was our source of amusement.

Mentors

The most poignant memories of my youth are my conversations with Andy Pasavanto, an Italian immigrant who was our janitor. All the apartment buildings had a janitor. They always lived in the basement apartment, and were paid little, but had free rent. They kept the vestibules (hallways of the building) clean and they shoveled the coal off the coal trucks into the basement, for the furnaces that heated the radiators in the apartments. It was an extremely tough job.

I have vivid memories of coming home in the winter, covered with snow, after bellyflopping for hours on the streets with my sled, and this sweet man, always dirty from the coal, and who had the smell of perspiration from an honest day's work, would see me in the entrance to the building and look at me with his kind eyes, and say, "Kenny, go to college, my boy. It's the only thing that no one can take away from you. Money, you can lose. Health, you can lose. But the knowledge, no one will ever take from you." He pointed to his head. I still visualize him doing that, pointing to his head. Andy Pasavanto was a very great man and his son Johnny went on to become an engineer and then an attorney. I know that, because one of my old neighbors, whom I ran into after fifty years at a class reunion, told me that she worked for a law firm as a receptionist in Phoenix and a man walked in and announced himself as Johnny Pasavanto, attorney. Andy would be proud.

Another mentor of mine was Maurie Andes, who owned Maurie's hot dog stand near Roosevelt High School. I ate lunch there every day.

The word cholesterol was unknown. Maurie put two sons through Harvard University from his hot dog stand. When I was older and driving a cab, working my way through undergraduate school, and wondering if I would survive, I would stop at Maurie's hot dog stand. He would instantly lift my spirits by inspiring me and telling me I will make it. Maurie always had a sweet smile and a kind word for everyone.

Teenage Years and Scars from Adolescence

In my third year of high school, I was thrown out of Roosevelt. All of my grades were either failing or barely passing, and I never attended school five days a week. I took off on Monday or Friday each and every week. I really hated school. When I was expelled (my permit revoked), I had to go to Tuley High School.

There are no words to describe how depressed I was that I had to go to Tuley. For one thing, I was one of the few Jews at that school, whereas Roosevelt was 90% Jewish. Tuley was extremely rough, like a reform school. On my first day, I literally saw a student throw a teacher down the stairwell. She came back three days later wearing a knee brace.

There was another young thug who got thrown out with me; his name was Norman Prokopow. On the first day that we were to report to Tuley, I walked to his house, which was about two miles away, so that we could go to Tuley together. I was that depressed.

Out of desperation, I called Roosevelt High School and begged the principal to take me back. I told him that I would do anything to get back. He told me that if I maintained a B average or above for one semester at Tuley, he would take me back. He also told me I couldn't have more than a couple of absences and no tardies. I got A's and B's and didn't miss one day. I was taken back to Roosevelt in my senior year. However, because I had not attended any summer schools for all the math classes that I failed, I had to do an extra semester before I graduated. I graduated second to the last in my class out of 175 students, and only Bob Ginsburg beat me out for last place. I could have cared less. I was convinced I would never go to college.

I am certain beyond a reasonable doubt that the reason I hated school is because of what happened to me when I was ten years old and in the fifth grade. My mother decided that she and I would take a vacation and go to California and stay with her second cousin (whom she barely knew) in the small town of Los Alamitos, a very poor town. We were to stay only for one month during summer vacation. Instead, we stayed for an entire semester and they enrolled me in a tiny grammar school where I was the only student who was not Hispanic. Ninety percent of the students did not wear shoes, and I was referred to as "City Slicker." I hated Los Alamitos with all my heart and I truly missed my friends. This experience for me at ten years old was one of the saddest I had ever had. Unfortunately for me, they were studying math that was far advanced from what I had been taught. They were doing fractions, and I had never been beyond simple division problems. I was completely lost, and all I did the entire semester in the math class was look out the window. This was the beginning of the end for me as a student. From that point on, I was never again interested in school until I entered college. I decided to just mark time until I got out. Too bad, I was too shy to discuss the problem with the teacher or with my mother and I paid for this dearly.

I bought my first car from Bennie Frum, a 1947 Hudson. Bennie was a character out of Damon Runyon. He was one of a kind, and he owned a car dealership on Western Avenue, which was a street that was filled with new and used car dealers. I became friendly with him. My friend Jerry Starkman and I decided that we wanted to make some money when we were seniors in high school. What we did was we went to Bennie Frum, and we bought cars really cheap on consignment. Then we ran ads in the paper and we sold them. We made more money than we ever dreamed. One day my friend Earl Pick decided to buy a car from Bennie, and Earl's father went to Bennie's car lot and bought the car. When he asked Bennie for the pink slip, Bennie said, "Pink slip? What is it with all this paper work? I'm getting sick of all this paper work. All I want to do is sell cars. I'm just going to have to get out of this business and find something else."

While I was growing up on Division Street, there were certain rituals that my friends and I would engage in. One was meeting outside of Michelov's Drug Store every Wednesday night. Starkman worked there as a pharmacist assistant and soda jerk and we waited for him to get off duty so we could go to the night races at the racetrack. Starkman would give us all free chocolate phosphates. If we didn't go to the racetrack, we went out to eat. One night, we arrived at an Italian smorgasbord. It was Dino, Starkman, Mitch, Ackerman, Becker, and I. As we walked in, they were closing. We sat down at a table, and the waitress said, "Sorry, but we are closed." Without missing a beat, Dino said, "How could we be here if you're closed?" Dino was like Aristotle.

Cooper and Cooper had a very long stainless steel counter and only stools to sit on, no booths. Eddie was the waiter at this short order restaurant, where all of us met after our dates. He was a real character and a great guy. He was extremely skinny. He was an ex-Navy man; a veteran who had tattoos all over his arms. He liked all of the boys. When we walked in, he always called us by our names. He asked us what was new in our life; what was going on. If anyone was short on money for chili, he would keep a tab for us. He was about fifteen years older than us and we looked up to him. We looked forward to seeing him there.

All the boys would meet here after our dates about 1 a.m. to discuss life. We had a "chili bowl," as Ed called it. It was forty cents.

After we had the chili, all the boys would pile into one of our cars, discussing our hopes and dreams and frequently lamenting about why our fathers had such a hard life, since they were such good men. These philosophical discussions were good for the soul and I still miss them.

When I was about fifteen years old, and my sister was eight, my mother hired a babysitter for her. Her name was Helen Pabitchik. She was a Polish immigrant and was not very sophisticated. I recall very vividly coming home from playing baseball and seeing her in our living room watching TV with her mouth wide open. TV was to her an extraordinary thing and she just looked like she was hypnotized when she watched. Also, she had a lot of dental problems, and I remember that my mother wanted to help her, financially, to get her teeth fixed. She told my mother not to worry because her father told her he would have all her teeth pulled out to save the maintenance.

When I was a teenager, all the cool boys would wear leather jackets made by Grace. We'd always have the collar up. We had long hair, Tony Curtis style, and we would have a d.a. (duck's ass, which means a line down the back of your hair). We also would have pegged pants. They were called draped and pegged, which means that the entire leg was ballooned out, but when it got down to the ankles, it was real tight; that was the peg. That's the way we dressed. We also wore "Mr. B collars." These collars were created by the great black soul singer, Billy Eckstein. He was handsome, smooth, and known for his high rolled-over collars, and even today, I still wear Mr. B collars, but I have them custom-made. They are my trademark. When I got ready to go out on the weekend, my apartment was always the meeting place. All my friends would come to pick me up. Sometimes I'd have five guys waiting for me. Before I could leave the house, my hair had to be perfect. I'd stand before the mirror with a comb. We used to use wildroot crème oil in our hair. "Use Wildroot Crème Oil, Charlie" was how the commercial ditty went. It was just sticky and gooey, but that was the only thing that kept it in place. My father used to mimic me when I stood in front of the mirror. I had all kinds of mirrors that I used to check the back of my hair. It was a very touching thing when my father used to turn each way in front of the mirror just like I did. When we'd leave the apartment, my friends would have to stand in front of me to block the wind before we got in the car so as not to mess my hair up.

I was in a club in high school called the Cavaliers. We called it a social and athletic club, but in reality, it was a club of rebellious, tough boys. Aside from having street fights, the guys in the club were decent guys, just a little misguided. Our president was Mike Takeman. I ran into him at our fortieth reunion, and he is a brain surgeon in San Francisco. Some of the other guys also did very well. Al Becker, prominent attorney; Al Ackerman, prominent attorney. Some of them just dropped out of sight. We had Leonard Juglarsky, he was a Polish kid, very big, and he looked like Robert Mitchum. He ended up being a longtime police officer with the Skokie Police Department. We had a counselor whose name was Don Paul. He was a psychology student at the time, and ended up getting a Ph.D. in psychology and also became an attorney, and eventually a public defender for Cook County. Everybody in the high school feared the Cavaliers. There were many clubs in the school: There were the Torpedoes, the Rockets, the Little Gentlemen, the Dappers, but the Cavaliers were the most feared. We wore red club jackets, with white lettering, and when anyone would see us with our club jackets, they would clear the aisles.

The Ferdlach and the Hurt

Ferdlach is Yiddish for horses. I was exposed to horse racing before I started kindergarten. My father used to take me.

My father referred to the racing form as "the bishop." I don't know why. I learned to handicap: to compare the different horses in class, won/loss record, age, speed, and how they do on a hard track or a soft track.

My father had a favorite line, "When you bet fast, you can't last. When you bet slow, you gotta go."

He would also tell people that the white flag that flew above the track was his shirt that he lost.

All of my father's friends were compulsive racetrack gamblers. A common sight was watching six of them pile into a car and head off to Maywood or Sportsmen's Park, where they would lose their rent money. Watching my father scream at the top of his lungs, "Come on, you pig," made me think he would die of a heart attack. When he lost big, he would sweat and shake. When I would ask how he did, he would always say, "I broke even." When he said that, I knew the rent money was gone, and then he would go to the "juiceman."

The juiceman did not serve beverages but would loan people money for 40% interest. If you did not pay when it was due, your legs would be broken. I was very insecure and frightened for the safety of my father.

I remember playing with my friends on the street at about twelve years old and two men jump-started my father's 1948 Oldsmobile right in front of us. When I ran to stop them, they told me they were repossessing the car because my father did not make his payment. I was humiliated. On several occasions, big guys would come to our apartment threatening to take our furniture unless my father paid his juice. One day they did, in fact, take our piano.

Unfortunately, most of my friends and I also became compulsive gamblers. We would go to the night races almost every night. Once, I got into such heavy debt at the age of seventeen years that I held a sale in my apartment and sold my clothes and my beloved clarinet. I am proud to say I finally gave up gambling in my early twenties and I have not been to a racetrack since.

Politics and the Cops

The former Speaker of the House, Tip O'Neill, said, "All politics are local." Boy, was he right. The Chicago political hierarchy begins with precinct captains. They serve as assistants to the powerful aldermen who run the city, along with the mayor. Unlike Los Angeles, whose mayor has very limited power, the Chicago mayor has almost dictatorial power. None more so than Mayor Richard Daly, Sr., and now his son Richard Daly, Jr. The aldermen are Chicago's version of the L.A. City Council, but much more powerful. The city is carved up into wards, and each ward has an alderman. Their assistants were called precinct captains.

No alderman was more powerful than the late Tom Keane, who was Mayor Daly's right-hand man. Of course, he was Irish, along with Daly, as were most of the powerful politicians in Chicago. Together, along with the powerful Jake Arvey (chairman of the Democratic Party and owner of one of the largest construction companies in Chicago), their Democratic machine put John Kennedy in the White House. Alderman Keane was eventually indicted and went to the joint. My sweet mother used to write to him. She had been his manicurist. She showed me letters from him.

The revered Jewish immigrant, Judge Irving Landesman, served on the bench for twenty-seven years and was Alderman Keane's secretary from the age of seventeen to thirty-seven, when he was finally rewarded with a judgeship. He became the Jewish version of the Godfather. He was loved by all and would help everyone.

Many young boys would receive jobs from their alderman such as picking up leaves in the park or other patronage jobs such as working at the Department of Water and Power, where you could eventually retire with a comfortable pension if you stayed twenty-five years.

The cops were 98% crooked. No, 99%. When I started driving at sixteen, my father gave me a two-dollar bill (a deuce), which was used at racetracks in those days. He told me to keep it in my wallet for when the cops stop me. At least once a week, I would get pulled over. I had done nothing. The cop would just look at me, and I would slip him the deuce and he would say thanks and leave. It didn't even occur to me that some cops were honest. This was all we knew.

Kenneth N. Green

Max Solomon, Dino's father, refused to be a part of the graft. Every time he got stopped by a cop, instead of giving the cop the deuce, Max would accept the ticket, and spend an entire day at the courthouse fighting it. He always lost, but he said, "It was the principle of the thing." My father would say, "Max, don't be a shmuck, and forget the principle so you don't lose a day's work."

One night a bunch of the boys, Dino, Johnny Walker, Starkman, and I, were driving around. Starkman wanted to show us some vending machines he bought, which were being stored in a garage in an alley pending placement in gas stations. It was around 2 a.m., and as we were leaving the garage, walking back to our car, another car zoomed up, and three tough-looking men got out and told us to stand facing a brick wall and put our hands up. I did exactly as we were told because I knew they were "the man." They patted us down and Starkman said, "Who are you?" One of them said, "Shut the fuck up." Starkman said, "If you are police, do you have a warrant?" The copper said, "Here it is," and Starkman went down from a short right to the chin. You don't mess with Chicago cops.

T.V. Star - Robert Conrad and Me

My Grammar School - "Von Humboldt"

**The Author - Far Right - Age 16 (1954) working at
Sammy's Hot Dog Stand on Division St.
Far Left - "Dino" Donny Solomon
In the Middle - Mitch Cohen**

The Shlub's Apartment Building

Left - Miguel Espino - #4 Middleweight Contender
Right - John Bray - 3 Time National Heavyweight Champ
Middle - The Author

The Old Galitsianer Shul - Now a Greek Orthodox Church

HALL MONITORS

HALL MONITORS

The hall monitors do a great service to the school in assisting with hall order and safety for all children. They are the traffic policemen of our school organization.

Miss O'Malley, our Assistant Principal, is in charge of this group. She selects them and assigns them to their posts. Only pupils with good scholastic and deportment records are eligible to serve on this assignment. All of you should cooperate with them in maintaining order and safety.
(The picture to the left, as well as the others in this issue were furnished us by Flanders Fotos).

GOSSIP COLUMN

FLASH: In the K-A-D-K newsroom we have just gotten some news hot off the teletype -
Mr. Kula, who was the teacher in Room 306, has a new teaching job at the Schneider School, and Mrs. McGovern has taken his place.

Miss Jahns, the teacher of Room 205, left Von Humboldt to teach at the Sayre School, and Mrs. Hennessy has been assigned to that room.

The girls of rooms 316, 317 and 301 went to visit Lucy Flower High School. P.S. Mr. Rosenthal was the only man teacher there.

Miss Chuchat is taking the girls of rooms 317 and 301 for girls' chorus.

We collected $81.35 at the White Elephant Sale.

Richard Rojeck of Room 301 plays the saxophone.

Room 301, 8A

Jean Wapner

HOME MECHANICS COOKING

If there are any people who would like to be future chefs, read this article, because in our school we have a place to learn how to cook - Home Mechanics.

Our head chef is Mr. Kral who seems to be at home in the kitchen. He has taught us to make poached eggs, cereals, hot cocoa, stewed prunes and cookies.

Our mouths are watering for more of his tasty dishes.

Room 316, 8B

Gerald Lee Zaidman

AN UNUSUAL OCCUPATION

My uncle has an unusual occupation. He is an inventor. He made a new plastic which is used by all the dentists. His occupation is unusual because he has no factory at all, but mixes the plastic on his wife's kitchen stove and fills the plastic in small jars and sells it to the dentists in every state in the United States. It is important that the dentists have this plastic. I think this is a very unusual occupation because it is carried on at home.

Room 215, 4A

Sheldon Sandack

SPRING

Spring is the season that everyone likes,
You see kids playing and riding bikes.
Everyone's happy and everyone's gay,
All this can happen on a nice spring day.

Room 302, 7B

Vicki Thomasson

I WONDER

I wonder how the lights outside turn off after night?
Because they aren't on when it's light!
I wonder how the moon knows when the sun's work is done?
To float about in heaven,
Must be fun!
I wonder how the roses bloom so red,
Everytime I look at them they seem to nod their head!

Room 118, 5A

Patricia Robinson

The Author - 2nd row from top, 3rd from right

VON HUMBOLDT GRADUATES

ROOM 317

Front Row (L to R) Rosalie Rosenthal, Marlene Renville, Lusi Barchuk, Janet Levy, Carol German, Barbara Gordon, Charlotte Rakowski, Marjorie Billings

Second Row - Lois Groebli, Ida Hansen, Mary Heath, Phyllis Berman, Phyllis Kobylinski, Jeanette Kolodziej, Rita Smelte

Third Row - Richard Relaz, Sherwin Chasen, Kenneth Green, Nyles Nelson, Roger Schwartz, Donald Kernes, Theodore Magura, Anthony Tselepis

Fourth Row - Donald Solomon, William Hausman, William Shlifka, Robert Phillips, Julius Marut, Raymond Bryszek

Fifth Row (Top) Louis Rowitz, Chester Komperda, Harold Walat, Ivars Freimanis, Nick Berley

The Author - 3rd row from top, 3rd from left

40

CLASS OF JUNE 1951

Flanders Foto

ROOM 301

Front Row (L to R) Loretta Duszaki, Ruth Smedberg, Bernadine Sogolow,
Dolores Lach, Donna Schroeder, Constance Radosta, Doris Farar, Iris Passen
Second Row - Stella Pelozaraka, Fern Farkash, Joan Lameka, Hazel Tatson,
Olga Paulike, Jean Wapner, Patricia O'Brien, Josephine Stecki
Third Row - Philip Coutee, Philip DeMatteo, Vernon Roe, Paul Reibman,
Bernard Swerdloff, Leon Fullett, Donald Talkowsky, Robert Relaz
Fourth Row - Betty Smoron, Domenica Shurba, Gerald Peskin, Willard Nachbin,
Mitchell Cohen, David Krzak, John Juraszek
Fifth Row (Top) Tomas Zummo, William Cohen, Richard Rojek, Bernard Ginsberg,
Stephen Lukashevich, Edward Komperda

Mitch Cohen - 2nd row from top, 3rd from right

Kenneth N. Green

The Boys

Mitch Cohen

Still my closest friend. The best street fighter in Chicago. A Jewish Rocky Graziano. Mitch fought at least three times a week whether he needed to or not, and never lost. To this day, he doesn't know why he fought so much. He's only five foot nine, but a natural athlete. He looks like an Irishman with blonde hair.

A riot broke out at one of our high school basketball games and the newspaper photographer caught Mitch dropping a huge guy with a short right to the guy's chin. This photo appeared on the second page of the *Chicago Sun Times* in 1953.

One day, Mitch and Dino and I were playing basketball at St. Fidelis basketball court. This was an outdoor cement court. Mitch got into a shoving match with a boy who was older and at least four inches taller and much heavier. His name was Mervyn Dukat. Mitch chopped down Dukat like a lumberjack chops down a tree. Mitch's punches were short and very powerful, like Joe Louis. Each time his heavy-handed punches landed on Mervyn's face, it made the same sound that a hammer would make when striking a watermelon. After what seemed like forever, Mervyn turned and walked away. I felt very sorry for him. Many years later, Mitch and I learned that Mervyn's father was the very feared gangster Harry Brown. Oh well!

Another one of Mitch's famous fights was with Al Scher. Scher was right out of a James Dean movie. He was always telling us that he had to prove himself and that he was a great fighter. One day, Scher and Mitch and Dino and Becker and I were having hot dogs at Maurie's Hot Dog Stand. Mitch took a French fry from Scher and all hell broke loose. They started to fight and the fight moved outside into an empty lot. It was perhaps the most brutal fight in unrecorded history. Blood was everywhere, but they wouldn't stop. As tough as Mitch was, Scher was his equal. It was Graziano versus Zale, all over again. After they had fought for about twenty minutes nonstop, Scher was on top of Mitch and finally getting the better of him. Mitch would never allow anyone to beat him, and so he decided it was time to end this fight. With his left hand, he reached out and grabbed a rock, and cracked Scher in the head, and that was the end of the fight. For many years later, Scher always referred to his killer headache that would never go away.

Mitch's parents were the age of my grandparents when he was born. They were good, hard-working people from Russia who could barely speak English. At home, they spoke only Yiddish. Mitch and I have been best friends since kindergarten. He and his wife Barbara and their grown children live in Orange County, California, and we call each other every day. He is a CEO for a cosmetic company. In junior college, Mitch took a course in zoology. One of the questions was, "What is an isomere?" Mitch's answer: "It is the opposite of vayosmere." *Vayosmere* in Yiddish means "Why me?"

When his sons reached adulthood, I told them that their father was the toughest Jew who ever lived. They looked at me with wide eyes and were totally astonished that he even knew how to fight because he is not a poster boy anymore for physical fitness. Mitch and Barbara are world-class parents. Their sons revere them.

Donny "Dino" Solomon

We were like brothers growing up—inseparable. His parents—Ruth and Max—were Russian immigrants and were best friends with my parents. I named him Dino. It just seemed to fit. We were watching the movie *Somebody Up There Likes Me* starring Paul Newman, which was the life story of the famous middleweight champion, Rocky Graziano. His buddy in the film was a kid named Dino, played by Sal Mineo. As we were leaving the theater, I said to Donny, who looked like the old movie actor Broderick Crawford, "From now on, you are Dino," and so he was. By the way, Dino's other nickname was "the Moon," because his face was indeed as round as the moon.

Dino had the most promise of all my friends: brilliant at math, a tremendous athlete, all the girls liked him, and all the boys respected him. He was strong as a bull, a natural leader.

One day, Dino and Mitch and Shelly Goodman and I were all working together at Sammy's Hot Dog Stand. Goodman had a red strawberry on his face from birth. He was a good-looking kid, but half of his face was bright red and I'm sure that affected him his entire life. Poor Shelly died last year of cancer. Shelly began talking about Dino's girlfriend, Adrianne. Goodman made a negative remark about her that caused Dino to utter his prophetic comment, which to this day all of us recite: "If you ever mock me or my broad again, I will kill you." Goodman backed off.

Like my father, Dino's father Max was an inveterate gambler. Our fathers went to the racetrack at least four times a week and lost all their money. Like me, Dino got addicted to gambling. He and I and about six of our other friends went to the night races (harness) almost every night as teenagers.

When we were sixteen, Dino started getting strange, really strange. He had broken up with his steady, Adrianne, which he took very badly. He quit the basketball team. He started coming home straight from high school every day and just sat around in his bedroom in his shorts, with an occasional break to sit at the kitchen table and cut a slice or two of hard salami (on an angle per orders from his mother, so "it would last longer").

His parents never turned the lights on until it was pitch dark, to save the money. Also, the radiator was kept off in the winter. Dino would spend most of his time sitting at the edge of his bed twirling the threads on the end of the bedspread. He twirled miles of thread. There was no TV in this house; only a radio tuned to the horse race results. We were never allowed to change the radio station. It would have been bad luck.

Dino worked in a Nabisco cracker factory at night when the plant was empty. He sat all alone at a desk with an adding machine doing accounting work. The rest of the boys and I would come over late at night to pick him up to go to the racetrack and catch the last two races for free.

One summer, when he had just started to get crazy, all of us slept overnight at the Shlub's apartment. Shlub's mother was on vacation for a week; she used to go to a resort area called South Haven Michigan, where all the Jewish women used to go. She left him home alone. So Mitch, Dino, Becker, and I spent several nights at the Shlub's apartment. All of the apartments were extremely hot during the summer. There were no air conditioners, but the Shlub's mother had a big oscillating fan by the window and like most families she'd put a large container of ice water near the fan so it would cool off the room. When Shlub wasn't looking, Dino urinated in the water, and that's what the Shlub's mother found when she came home from vacation.

Dino was like a cat—he had to establish his territory. So not only did he pee in the bowl of ice water by Shlub's fan, but he frequently peed in the huge wooden barrel that held the piccalilli at the hot dog stand where we worked. To this day, I don't eat piccalilli.

Another crazy thing that Dino did was, when we were all were at Becker's tiny apartment while Becker's father was working at the bar that he owned. It was Becker, Dino, Zaidman, Mitch, and I. There was a young kid named Mike who lived down the street and he used to look up to us. Mitch told him that we had a girl in the apartment and he could have sex with her. He came up to Becker's apartment, and he started to get undressed, and Mitch told him that the girl was in the bedroom under the sheets. When he walked into the bedroom and pulled down the sheets he saw Dino, and Dino gave him the hideous face. When Dino started getting crazy, he would do what we'd call the hideous face. We'd always say, "Dino, give us the 'hideous face.'" He would contort his face like a monster. Anybody would be frightened if they saw it. Sometimes he'd just be walking down the street and he'd give some poor person the hideous face and they would be terrified.

When we graduated from high school, Dino said to me, "Why don't we join the Army on the buddy system, we will be the first two Jewish generals?" Like a dope, I went for it. More later.

Eddy Stark

Eddy was strong as a bull from shlepping izon, carrying iron. Eddy was not my closest friend, but we did shoot hoops together at least three times a week, when he would pick me up in his 1941 Ford. He had an extremely hard life. He started working on his father's junk truck (scrap iron and metal) when he was twelve years old. Every day after high school, he would work with his father in the truck, except for the forty-five minutes beforehand when we would play basketball. One day, his father died in his arms after getting caught up in a machine that straps metal around wastepaper. His father's head was crushed.

Jerry Freeman

Jerry Freeman is now a multimillionaire and the owner of Gulliver's Italian Restaurant in Skokie. When we were kids, Jerry couldn't make change for a nickel. Now his restaurant contains priceless antiques and artwork. Jerry was a very heavy stutterer, and couldn't get through a sentence without repeating each word five times. Fortunately, he was also drop-dead gorgeous, and the ladies loved him. We called him "Ruberosa," after the famous Latin lover, Porfirio Ruberosa, of the 1950s.

Al Becker

Becker looked like Tonto of *The Lone Ranger*. He was the darkest-complected Jew you would ever see. His mother died when he was two, and his father died when he was sixteen. Raised by his aunt and uncle, Becker is a very prominent and wealthy Chicago attorney. Becker rose to become a full partner in a very prestigious law firm. It was predictable, because Becker was the only one of us who took Latin in high school and always enjoyed opera.

His father was a great man and used to take Al and me to dinner frequently. His father called Al "Arie," which was his Hebrew name.

Because I received failing grades in algebra two years in a row, I was told to go to summer school at Lane Tech, a tough, boys-only school. I would register every summer, but never attended class. Instead, I would go to Becker's apartment at 7:00 a.m., where his father would let me hide out until the afternoon.

Al Ackerman (Johnny Walker)

He became one of the most prominent criminal defense attorneys in Chicago. Johnny was brilliant. He always walked around with an umbrella, hence the name Johnny Walker, which I gave him, because he looked like the character on the Scotch bottle. He had an extremely high pompadour for his hairstyle, and he was only able to keep it that way because he wouldn't wash his hair for a year. He held the world's record for not washing his hair, and I came in second, because I would wash mine twice a month. He also wore Mr. B collars like I did, high up on the neck and rolled, and he was also a high school champion wrestler in the lightweight division. Additionally, he had a great build and was a weightlifter. Now he tells me that his clients are either dead, have beards, or are in the joint. We have been friends for fifty years. Every few months he calls me to say hello. Johnny: "Cousin Kenny—it's Cousin Johnny." Johnny's mother, Ann Ackerman, was a big mucky-muck in the Democratic Party, and in fact, toward the end of her life she was the cochairman of the presidential campaign for Michael Dukakis. Ann was also very active in the NAACP and was on their board of directors. Of all of my friends' mothers, she was the most literate and politically astute and involved in the community.

On any given night, one would find Ackerman studying at the neighborhood laundromat while he was in law school. "It relaxes me."

Jack Lazar (Mingo Rip)

Mingo was crazy from the day he was born. He used to talk about molesting his infant niece and wanting to have sex with his sister. One day at an assembly in high school he took out a knife and buried it deep in another student's leg because he thought it would be fun. He shot a kid in the leg on the basketball court. He became a heroin addict and joined the Army Airborne, and when he got out, he became a courier for some corporation driving a bicycle delivering things. When I came home from Korea, Mingo started coming over to my apartment. Within weeks of my return from the service, my father told me that he had a big problem. He and some of his men painted a building that was owned by a disbarred attorney named Morris Teitlebaum, aka Maurice. Teitlebaum had been an attorney for the mob. He would not pay my father for the job. I told my father that I would go to Teitlebaum's office and try to get the money. Mingo offered to go with me and somehow we got into the office and Mingo gave Teitlebaum the mad-dog look. Teitlebaum wrote me a check on the spot.

Several years ago when I was in Chicago on a visit, Jack's ex-wife Phyllis told him that I was at the Ambassador East hotel. I hadn't spoken to him in about thirty-five years. I answered the phone and he said,

47

"This is Jock." I said, "Who is Jock?" I recognized his voice. Finally, I said, "Is this Jack Lazar?", and he said yes. He asked me if I had any cocaine. Me: "I don't do cocaine, I'm a Jewish lawyer and I'm not into the bullshit." That was my last conversation with Mingo Rip. He died last year of a heart attack. Mingo was truly damaged goods.

Gerry Zaidman

His mother and father came from Poland and his father abandoned the family when Gerry was twelve years old. Gerry's mother never wanted alimony or child support. Gerry became a CPA and had as his clients, among others, the mayor of Chicago. He and his wife Brenda still live on the outskirts of Chicago. A stand-up guy; we talk on the phone all the time and spend time together on my yearly visits. Gerry is a wonderful and dear friend and one of the most decent guys who ever lived. I would put Zaidman at the top of my list of people that I would want to be in a foxhole with.

I was one of the first of the boys to drive a car in high school. I used to pick Zaidman up in my father's 1948 Oldsmobile and we drove together to high school. On the way home, we would always get in an argument, and I would pull over, and we would get out and fight. When we finished, I would drive him home, and pick him up the next day.

Jerry Starkman

Jerry Starkman is a lovable guy and we've been friends all our lives. Jerry is very short and he has a habit of standing on his tiptoes and rubbing his hands together whenever he has made a good business deal. One of the things that stand out in my mind is that when I left Chicago and drove out to California with Gartzman and Dino, I had left behind my beautiful 1955 Chevy convertible. It was like brand new, customized; it was the most beautiful car. When I decided not to return to Chicago, I called Starkman and I told him I needed a favor, because he was in the business of selling cars, among other things. I asked him if he'd please sell my car, and I found out that he just left it parked on a corner collecting tickets, because I was getting the parking tickets in the mail. I was dead broke. I was attending college, living with my father, mother, and sister in L.A. My father was broke. I was getting these parking tickets for $20 a pop. I must have gotten fifty of them. They kept coming and coming and coming. And my father told me I had to pay them, because if I came back to Chicago they'd arrest me, and he was right. Also, I was thinking of becoming an attorney, and I didn't want to ruin my reputation. I kept writing Starkman letters and begged him to park my car legally, but he ignored them. Finally, I wrote him and told him I was coming to get him, and I was going to cripple him. Years later, I forgave him. He told me that he didn't mean any harm, and that Becker, who was an attorney, told him don't worry about it, so Starkman thought he didn't have to worry about it.

Rita Springer was the niece of Nate the barber. Rita was one of the most beautiful girls in Chicago, just stunning, tall, and slim—a Sharon Stone look-alike. Starkman married her when she was about nineteen. Starkman was about twenty-five. Their marriage lasted long enough to produce two sons and they got divorced when the sons were young boys. Rita moved to Florida and met a Cuban medical doctor who made a lot of money. He adored Rita and was extremely jealous. They had a beautiful home and on the front lawn he had a statute made of Rita in the nude. Eventually, Rita and the doctor decided to get a divorce and during the time pending the divorce, the doctor called her one night and told her to meet him at a local restaurant to discuss the settlement. During the discussion the doctor pulled out a gun and started shooting at her. She ran, and was hit by about five bullets, and died at the scene. The doctor then turned the gun on himself and shot himself dead in the head. Everyone who knew Rita was devastated because she was a beautiful, decent, nice young woman. Their children were raised without a mother and Starkman did a wonderful job. Recently, my sister was going through some of my mother's old letters. One of the letters was from Rita's mother to my mother, which was written just six months before Rita was killed. Rita's mother Shirley told my mother, "I am very worried for the safety of my daughter and I'm afraid of this crazy doctor that she is married to."

Starkman never went past high school but became a multimillionaire. He owns Mustard's Last Stand, a famous hot dog stand adjacent to Northwestern University. He owns other businesses as well. Jerry's father walked out on him when he was an infant, and his sweet mother Sally raised him by herself. She was from Poland. Starkman and I are still tight.

Shelly Zuchman (The Shlub) (Yiddish for Big Slob)

Right out of Damon Runyon. A true dees, dems, and dose guys. We had been friends since kindergarten. He never finished high school and bought a pawnshop on the South Side.

The Shlub had a grandmother who was about three feet tall. Her name was Rose and she spoke only Yiddish. She and the Shlub were always yelling at each other and whenever that happened, he would grab her by the arm and push her into a closet and lock the door. He would not let her out for at least a couple of hours. She would cry, and he would say, "You're being punished." God forgive him.

The Shlub was constantly telling my father that he would quit high school and become rich by owning a pawnshop. My father laughed and said, "You quit high school, but Kenny will go to college and law school and become an attorney." Shelly did not become rich, and I did become a lawyer. Thanks, Dad.

Earl Pick

Although Earl was not from Division Street, I include him because he is a dear friend. We became friends when I was fourteen years old and going to Roosevelt High School on a permit before I got thrown out. Roosevelt High School was in a middle-class area, called Albany Park, on the North Side, and that was where Earl lived. I always thought that he was rich, although he wasn't. His father merely made a living. But I definitely came from the wrong side of the tracks (ten miles south) compared to where he lived.

When I told him I was writing this book, he said, "Don't forget to include the question that you asked me when we were teenagers." The question was, "Did your father ever play catch with you?" My father never played catch with me, but Earl looked like the kind of kid that would have had that experience. I also asked him if his father smoked a pipe and owned slippers.

I had another friend in the neighborhood. He was the son of my mother's close friend, Rose Bartnick, and her husband Kye, who was an optician. This boy's name was Dickie Bartnick. Dickie was a wild kid. He was very hyper and I never felt comfortable around him. He died at the age of twenty-five on a toilet seat, after overdosing on heroin. I would see him from time to time because my mother and his mother were so close. Rose and her husband were Polish. I found out after Dickie died that Rose had an ongoing affair with Nate the barber. The two couples used to go out, Nate and his wife, and Rose and Kye, and yet they were carrying on like that. Dickie was their only child. He was always involved in some craziness. He started driving at age sixteen. His father had a 1951 Mercury, with the long swoop back like the Batman car. Dickie used to go down the side streets at 80 mph and predictably, he killed a little three-year-old girl and dragged her for blocks. The neighbors were chasing him. They got his license number and they caught him. He ended up getting Nate to intercede on his behalf because Nate knew all the judges. Dickie served no time; he got probation. But everybody knew that Dickie was destined for some horrible life. Once Dickie and I had a fight near my apartment building during a rainstorm. It was raining so hard, you could barely see. I don't remember what caused the fight, but we fought for several hours. I got the best of him and he quit. He went home all bloody. His father came by the next day driving his Mercury up and down the streets looking for me. He had his wife Rose in the car, and when he finally found me, he said, "Why don't you and Dickie go into the boxing ring?" And I said, "That's great, you read my mind, that's exactly what I want to do." But of course, that never happened. Dickie Bartnick's best friend was Sydney Stevens. Everybody was afraid of Sydney. Sydney had white hair, and he just looked like he could kill you in a minute. I never had a problem with Sydney, but I steered clear of him because he looked psycho to me. He and Dickie were inseparable. They were always getting into trouble. Rose Bartnick had a really nice body, but she was one of the ugliest woman that God ever created. Her face could stop a clock. My father would call Rose "Doll Face."

There was a guy named Arnie Orleans who lived on my street. He was two years older than me and he was famous for one thing and that was constantly adjusting his balls while he stood on the streetcorner talking to other kids. Why did he do it? Only the Jewish God knows.

There was another guy who was a year older than I was and was a legend on Division Street, and his name was Freddy Rosen. Freddy was as tough as Mitch or maybe even tougher, and he was an outstanding athlete and was a member of every team at Roosevelt High School. To this day, Freddy still plays basketball with some of the star players, and they tour the entire city. Freddy's father owned a tiny liquor store when I was in high school named Sam's Liquors. This liquor store has moved several times and is now one of the largest retail liquor stores in the United States.

Gif Me Hadogs

I was hired the day I turned sixteen and got a work permit to work at Sammy's Hot Dog Stand. Dino and Mitch were also hired. I worked a minimum of thirty-five hours per week part time, for seventy-five cents an hour. I saved for my first car—a battleship grey 1947 Hudson with a tiny rear window that cost $200 and was solid steel and looked like an Al Capone car. This car holds the world record for spending more time in the shop than any other car. Every dime I made went into that car. I replaced every part. I worked in the hot dog stand until I went into the Army at age eighteen. I eventually earned $1.25 per hour. The owner was Sammy Feldman, who had a wooden arm because his real arm was shot off in WWII at Bastogne. Sammy would bet all the neighborhood boys that he could put his arm in the boiling French fry oil. None of them knew his arm was wooden and Sammy always won the bets.

The hot dog stand was small and was made of wood, and had a big awning in the front. There was a long stainless steel counter for the outdoor customers to stand in front of and place their order, and inside the hot dog stand were about ten stools with stainless steel counters at hand's level. The work area was very tiny and sometime on a busy day there were three of us working at one time serving hot dogs, and it's a miracle we didn't bump into each other. We would take the order and we would grab a hot bun from one of the bins, at the same time with our other hand pull a hot dog out of the boiling water with prongs, put the hot dog on the bun and then put the dressing on, which consisted of mustard, onion, piccalilli and hot peppers, as well as French fries, and I was so fast that I could prepare an entire sandwich and wrap it in about less than ten seconds. In the back of the hot dog stand without a door, we had an onion chopping machine, where we would skin the onion, put it on a grate, push the lever down, and it would chop the onion into tiny pieces, and when we did that, we would cry like babies. We also had a potato slicing machine, and we would first skin the potatoes and then place it in this machine and slice it into what looks like French fries.

On Friday I would start my shift at 5 p.m. and work until 4 a.m. Saturday morning. That is when the bars close in Chicago. On Saturday, I would start working at 5 p.m. and work until 5 a.m. Sunday morning when the bars close. I must have served 20 million hot dogs. Sometimes the lines were so long I couldn't see the end of it. I held the world's speed record for dressing and wrapping hot dogs and fries. Most of the customers were Polish immigrants and they would stand at the stainless steel counter and tap their quarter constantly until they would be waited on. I would say, "Can I help you?" They would say, "Gif me ha dogs." I would say, "How many ha dogs?" They would say, "Von ha dog."

One of the guys I worked with was big Harry Zwerling. Harry was one of the toughest Jews who ever lived and could rip a man's trache out if he so desired. On more than one occasion, some Puerto Rican hoodlums threatened me, and Harry would just look at them, and they would back off. Harry, I have been told, became a millionaire from his furniture business.

One day, one of my customers, a tough Puerto Rican, came in with a zip gun, and told me he would give it to me for frozen custard. I took the deal and the next day I went to the sporting good store and bought some 22-caliber bullets. I went home and closed the door in my bedroom and put the .22 shell into the wooden zip gun and pulled back the rubber band, which acted as a hammer, and the bullet went through the wall and just missed my mother who was ironing in the kitchen. I threw the zip gun in the trash.

The Army

Dino convinced me to join the Army one year after high school. We were wasting our time in junior college, getting poor grades and not attending classes.

Dino told me that if two guys volunteered for the draft together, the Army would keep them together on the "buddy system." He told me that we would be the first two Jewish generals. I was dumb and we signed up (volunteered for the draft) for two years and we were to report at the induction center downtown at 5 a.m. on February 5, 1957.

A number of the boys (Starkman, Mitch, Ackerman, and Becker) picked me up first at 3:00 a.m. I said goodbye to my parents and we drove to Dino's apartment building. It was cold and dark outside. All the lights were out in Dino's apartment, so we rang the bell. No answer. We began to throw pebbles at his bedroom window, but he never came out. Finally, we got his mother up, and we got Dino out of the apartment. We arrived at the induction center just in time to be put on a bus to go to Fort Leonard Wood, Missouri.

When we arrived, it was even colder than Chicago. We were greeted by the first sergeant, who was a giant black man about 6'4" and 250 lb. He was, we were told, an ex-professional football player.

Sergeant: "All you mother fuckers who think you are tough gangsters from Chicago will soon find out what tough is. We will shave off all your hair and you will no longer look like Elvis. And if you get smart, you will pay." I was not thrilled.

Dino and I had all our hair clipped off. The barber laughingly said, "Do you want it Elvis style?" We were assigned to different barracks. So much for the buddy system.

Basic training was very cold and very tough. For some reason, I drew more K.P. than any soldier in the United States Army. I scrubbed the grease pit from the mess hall; I washed trays and served chow. I had K.P. all the time even though we were supposed to be selected by alphabet. I also served guard duty more times than anyone in my company. I still don't know why.

But, where was Dino? I didn't see him for about a week. Finally, I asked a soldier in his barracks if he knew a soldier named Solomon. The soldier said that Solomon was a fireman. That would be someone whose sole job was to shovel coal into the furnaces. A few days later, while we were marching, I saw a white man with black face like Al Jolson, walking near the furnaces. He was shoveling coal. It was Dino. Dino could not handle basic training so they gave him that job.

When we finished our eight weeks of basic training, a sergeant who was to decide where we would do our second eight weeks of training interviewed us. Dino was first in line.

Sergeant: "Private, what did you do in civilian life?" Dino: "I went to high school and I worked in a hot dog stand." Sergeant: "You're going to Fort Sam Houston, Texas, to be a cook."

Sergeant (turning to me): "Private, what did you do in civilian life?" Me (smiling): "I went to the same high school, and worked in the same hot dog stand." Sergeant: "You will go to Fort Sill, Oklahoma, where you will be in the artillery." So much for the buddy system. Oh well!

After the second eight weeks, I did not even get a furlough, but was sent directly to Korea. Dino was discharged on a Section 8 (mental discharge under honorable conditions).

Dino wrote me that he fooled the shrinks. This was the beginning of the end for Dino.

I arrived in Korea in June of 1957. I had been trained in artillery to fire the eight-inch Howitzer and the 105 and 155 cannons. They didn't give us earplugs and I have had serious hearing loss ever since.

The day I got there, I was taken to a Quonset hut on a mountain near the D.M.Z.; this was to be my company. It was a Sunday and therefore no brass was around. Was I depressed. I knew that I had to serve sixteen and a half months here, because that was the tour of duty in those days.

I believed that I was the only city boy in Korea and the only Jew.

I took an empty top bunk and lied down and was reading a movie magazine that I had bought at the PX in Japan. Within about fifteen minutes, a redneck that came right out of the movie *Deliverance* approached me. Ron White's neck was bigger than my thigh. He was about six feet tall, and weighed about 230. I am 5'9" and at that time weighed only 150 lbs. He was every civilized man's worst nightmare.

This hillbilly had been drinking and decided that I would become his source of amusement. He came over to my bunk and asked me if I was from Chicago. I had told no one where I was from, so I surmised that he had seen my personnel file downstairs in headquarters. I tried to ignore him, but he was relentless. He kept coming back to my bunk, and began shaking it violently, and finally said, "What do people in Chicago do beside get run over by trucks and get shot at?" He then said, "Are you a Jew?" At that moment, I decided that I must kill him, because I knew I would not survive and I did not want my parents to get a letter that I had died in Korea the day I got there only because I was a Jew. He then said, "Where is your tail, Jew?" I grabbed for the knife in my mess kit that was hanging from my bunk, jumped off the bunk, and put the knife in his belly. To my surprise it went in, because it wasn't even a serrated edge. I twisted the knife in this animal's belly and got on top of him, but he was so strong that he pushed me off like I was a feather. He picked up an M-1 rifle and held it by the barrel and started swinging this nine pounds of metal at me. I started to run, but realized there was nowhere to go since we were in the middle of wilderness surrounded by rice paddies.

Suddenly the one black guy in my outfit—his last name was Maize—a 6'3" skinny guy, grabbed the hillbilly's arms from behind and told me to run. Instead, I came back, and continued to beat on him until he finally had no more fight left in him. He was taken to the hospital and stitched up. The next day, Monday, the first sergeant called me to his office. I thought I would be court-martialed. He asked me what happened and where I was from. I said Chicago. He said that he had taught ROTC in Chicago at Northwestern University, and smiled, and told me to have a nice day, and that was the end of it.

When Ron White got out of the hospital, I owned him. To this day, he must be telling his trailer-trash friends, "Never fuck with psycho Jews."

They assigned me a job climbing telephone poles and running telephone wires from pole to pole. My m.o. (job description) was 3-10, a lineman. Unfortunately, I was terrified of heights and after about one month I went to my first sergeant and told him I couldn't climb telephone poles anymore. I got a new job, telephone switchboard operator. I worked eight hours on and sixteen hours off.

My workstation was a tiny Quonset hut with a potbelly stove and a switchboard in the middle of nowhere nestled alongside a mountain. When the switchboard rang, I answered "Drake, sir," which was our code name, and I connected the officer on the other end of the line, by using a hand crank. Most of the time, I got electric shocks when cranking it.

The Quonset hut that I actually lived in had about ten or twelve men in it. The soldier who bunked next to me was a man named Frazier. He was the grandson of a famous industrialist who owned a steel company. He proudly told me, one day, that he had been Jewish but converted to Christianity. This turned my stomach. How could a Jew, just twelve years after the Holocaust, deny his heritage? What a punk.

One night, he had been to the village, partying and drinking mocklie juice (fermented rice). This stuff was so strong it could blind you. He came back late and drunk and fell asleep in his sleeping bag. It was winter and freezing cold; 20 degrees below zero not counting the wind chill factor.

I woke up in the middle of the night and pissed all over his sleeping bag. This was something I was compelled to do. In the morning when he awoke, he said, "Where did all these icicles come from?" Me: "The roof must be leaking."

We had no electricity for the first six months; we had to use candles for lighting. Our water came from the polluted stream, and we had to put pills in it so that it was drinkable, and we had no showers and had to bathe using water from a bowl until generators were finally installed to give us showers, which we were able to take twice a week.

O.K. Boychik, You Start Tomorrow

I came home from Korea at the age of nineteen. My wonderful father, who had not completed grammar school and who spoke broken English, waited about a week and then said, "Let's talk." Dad: "So vot are you going to do mit your life?" Me: "I'll be a house painter just like you." Dad: "Vouldn't you rather be a lawyer?" Me: "No. I barely graduated from high school and I never read a book, so how can I go to college?" Dad: "O.K. Boychik, you start tomorrow."

He had me painting closets in the black projects for two days and on the third day I said, "Pop, I'm going to be a lawyer." He smiled.

None of my friends, and I mean none, went away to college. That only happened in the movies. I had once mentioned it to my father and he looked at me as if I were crazy. Everyone I knew who did go to college started at Wright Junior College. They had to take dummy English because they didn't pass the entrance exam for college English. Although I never read a book before college, for some reason I was good in that subject, and did not have to take dummy English.

I told my father that I was sure that I would flunk out. "Wrong," he said. "You are very smart and you could be president." He always said, "Every man puts on his pants the same way."

I told him that I would take fifteen units (a full load, which was five courses) and I would pick one class and give it all I had. If I got an A, I would go all the way. I picked business law, and to my utter amazement, I was one of only two people in the entire class that got an A.

Because we had no money, I had to work two jobs. I sold cash registers part-time, for a sweet man named Harry who owned American Cash Register Company on Milwaukee Avenue. Harry paid me a flat $40 per week, plus commission. I would canvas neighborhoods every day after my college classes. I would average $100 a week with commission, because I was a hard worker. 100 dollars a week in 1959 was probably like $1,000 a week now. One day I walked into a liquor store. At least I thought it was a liquor store because it had liquor signs all over. The store was totally empty. The owner came up some stairs from the basement. This was no doubt a front for some illegal operation.

I also drove a Yellow cab on the weekends and made $50 per night, net. I would take the cab out Friday at 5 p.m. and drive til 4 a.m. Saturday morning when the bars would close. I had a world-class bladder and rarely stopped to use the bathroom. I would then go home to sleep and I would pick the cab up again at 5 p.m. on Saturday and drove until 5 a.m. Sunday when the bars would close. I would begin again on Sunday at 5 p.m. and drove til midnight. Sometimes, I also drove during the week.

This was a dangerous gig. My friend Mitch, who also drove a cab, was almost killed. He picked up two hoodlums who directed him to the South Side and into an alley, where they took his $7 and threw his shoes and car keys into the snow after they cut his neck with a knife.

I came close. I was driving down the Outer Drive by Lake Michigan about 2 a.m. when my passenger in the back seat said, "What would you do if I jacked you up?" Me: "Please don't. I just got home from Korea and I only have $5. If you give me a pass, you could go to my friend Shelly's pawn shop on 47th and Drexel and he will take care of you." He gave me a pass. I think he just let me go because he felt sorry for me. I never told Shelly and he never mentioned anyone using my name.

One day, I was parked at a cabstand, when two guys—right out of *The Godfather*—told me to roll down my window. They identified themselves as union reps for the cab company. The election for president of the Yellow cab union was next week. "Who youse gonna vote for?" they asked. Me: "Whoever you want me to." Reps: "Good boy. Vote for Joey Glimpko." And I did. I recall driving down deserted streets on Christmas with the snow falling and all the Christmas lights were on. I would wonder—why is my life so tough? No family here—all alone. I would frequently drive my cab to Roosevelt University and take a few classes and get back in the cab to make some money.

Somehow, with two jobs and going to full-time college, I graduated from Wright Junior College with an AA degree. To my mother and father, you'd think I'd graduated from Oxford.

I then entered Roosevelt University. It was downtown on Michigan Avenue in a brick building and one would never know it housed a college.

Non-Jews called Maxwell Street "Jew town." It was a long street of shops and it was impossible to walk down the street without being almost physically grabbed by a shopkeeper entreating you to buy his merchandise. It was fifteen minutes from Division Street by car. I bought my first suit on Maxwell Street for $29. It was a green pinstripe, and I had just come home from Korea and needed a suit for one of the boy's weddings.

Speaking of Maxwell Street, my father had 100 gallons of paint that he had bought from someone and asked me if I wanted to sell it on Maxwell Street for $1.98 a gallon. I obtained a permit by paying off the man who was in charge of permits. And I went with Dino and loaded up my father's half-ton truck and spent the day at Maxwell Street and we sold every can.

The Disintegration of My Family

In 1960, when I was twenty-two years old and a junior in college, my father decided that the family would move to Los Angeles. My poor

59

father had become an alcoholic and his painting business had all but evaporated. He and my mother and sister moved to Los Angeles, and I decided I was not going to leave Chicago. My roots were there. My dad's eight brothers and sisters offered to help him start up a paint store. He called it Ken's Paint Store because he had no credit and had to use my name under power of attorney. Later, I found out what a wicked instrument that was. My financial reputation could have easily been ruined, but my father didn't allow that to happen.

I lived alone in Chicago for a year and a half going to college and working two jobs. I was a taxi cab driver and I sold cash registers. I frequently drove my taxicab to Roosevelt University to take my classes and got back in the cab to go make a living.

Leaving Chicago for Los Angeles

I was still living in Chicago when my father invited me to attend a cousin's wedding in L.A. in 1962. I decided to take a short vacation and I drove there with my friend Dino and a fellow cab driver who had been my roommate, named Shelly Gartzman. We drove a new Cadillac to the new owner. When I left Chicago, it was one of the worst winters ever. It was January 1962 and it was freezing cold and snowing. When we arrived in L.A., it was a balmy 70 degrees and the streets were filled with palm trees.

Gartzman and I had shared a one-bedroom apartment in one of the worst areas of Chicago on Ardmore Street and our rent was $110 a month ($55 apiece). The beds came out of a wall and the kitchen consisted of a hot plate, a built-in refrigerator, and the toilet was so close to where we slept, that it was disgusting. Over our twin Murphy beds were plumbing pipes. When we got to L.A., I knew within a couple of days that I would remain in Los Angeles.

Gartzman was a full-time cab driver while I was a part-time cab driver and attended college full-time. Gartzman had an odor about him that was indescribable. He probably held the world's record for not bathing; also, he would sit at our little table at the kitchenette and make mustard sandwiches. He also would steal my orange juice. Gartzman was born old. When I lived with him I was twenty-two years old and he was about twenty-five, but he looked and acted like he was fifty. He was also a habitual gambler at the racetrack. The one time that I met his mother, he had asked me to go with him to his mother's apartment to pick something up. They were screaming at each other the entire time. It was an extremely dysfunctional relationship.

After being in LA for three days, I decided to stay.

As much as I loved the weather in L.A., I was totally mystified by the people. They were from another world than the people I grew up with. I took a girl named Judy to a party. She had been Miss La Jolla. We walked into the party and a big guy immediately grabbed her by the hand and started dancing with her. The guys from Division Street would have chopped off his hand, and so I decided to have a talk with him. Me: "Get your hands off of my girl. Didn't your father teach you any manners?" He got the message and walked away.

I enrolled at Cal State L.A. for my senior year of undergraduate school, and they took all my credits. I moved in with my mother, father, and sister in their tiny apartment and got a part-time job selling men's wear at the Broadway Department Store on Wilshire Boulevard.

Among other classes, I needed to take a required course in speech in order to graduate. I was terrified. I couldn't put a sentence together. I sounded like Muggs McGinnis from the Dead End Kids. Guys from Division Street "tawked" like this. Drama was pronounced "draama." Roof was pronounced "ruff." Route was pronounced "root." Sandwich was pronounced "sanawich." Barbed wire was "bobbed wire." Additionally, we had different names for different things, like soda was called pop, and movies were the show.

Although I got all A's on my written assignments in the speech class, when it was my turn to stand before the class and deliver a monologue, I failed miserably. Most of my classmates were drama and speech majors and they laughed as I struggled to sound normal. I felt helpless. When the professor gave me a D for a final grade, I approached him on campus and said, "Are you proud of yourself for not giving a break to someone who has a handicap?" He was a true punk.

Boxing and Why One Boxer is Worth More than 100 Lawyers

I sat on my father's knee listening to the radio when Joe Louis knocked out Max Schmeling in the first round of their rematch.

I was hooked. I constantly listened to many more fights on the radio before there was television.

Once there was television, the fights were a big part of my life. Every Friday night was the "Gillette Fight Night." Like many boys, I visualized myself as heavyweight champion of the world. I had lots of street fights growing up, but, like most boys, I didn't know how to box although I was strong.

When my son Joey was eight years old, he told me that he wanted to learn to box. He must have been the victim of a bully at school. I was glad that he didn't want to learn karate or kung fu or any of that other movie stuff like most kids did.

A few days after he expressed an interest in boxing, we were at the Nautilus gym at 5:45 a.m. working out as usual, when I observed the manager banging the heavy bag. I knew that he was a boxer. It takes a lot of skill to bang the heavy bag properly. Me: "Do you know where I can take my son for boxing lessons?" Manager: "You got lucky. There is an old Jewish guy on the next block who was a champion boxer and who teaches little boys to box."

After work that day, my son and I walked up the urine-smelling steps to the second floor of a boxing gym on Van Nuys Blvd. The gym was right out of the *Rocky* movie. Eventually, I met many world champions who trained there.

I introduced myself to Frankie Goodman—a tough, gruff, elderly Jewish boxer from Philadelphia, the city that produced some of the best fighters in the world, including Joe Frazier. The "Philadelphia Left Hook" was created there.

Frankie was "in the book." He was the former national lightweight champion (1936) and was selected to go to Berlin in the Olympics along with Jessie Owens. Frankie was picked to win the gold medal in boxing. However, the Anti-Defamation League contacted him and they begged him not to go in order to send a message to Hitler. Frankie, being a good Jew, refused to go, and regretted it for the rest of his life. He realized that withdrawal hadn't accomplished its intended purpose; better for a Jew to win, he later thought.

Frankie never made much money in boxing in spite of having two bachelor's degrees from Penn State and being a master boxer and superb teacher.

Frankie and I became close friends. He developed a system of teaching little boys to box by drilling a large hole in the boxing ring. He would get down in the hole, which would make him the same height as the boys, some of whom were as young as four. For a while, he had a TV show called "Kid Boxing."

Frankie: "Step in, step out. Move to the left, and keep your hands up at all times. Pick the jab or slip it. When you throw the jab, don't wait for the receipt, get it back quick. Where's the powa? Show me your powa." I still hear his words.

He taught defense first, spending months on it before he would teach them to throw a punch.

Frankie had the best left hook I ever saw. It was picture perfect and he was so good that he was in the Jewish Hall of Fame (the book) alongside great athletes like Sandy Koufax, Benny Leonard, Barney Ross, and Hank Greenberg.

Frankie would regale me with stories about the great fighters that he knew well, like Sugar Ray Robinson and Joe Louis. Frankie had also managed several world champions.

I began to get interested in learning to fight correctly and started training in his gym. Among many others who worked out there were heavyweight champ Michael Dokes; Tex Cobb, heavyweight contender; Randy Shields, who fought for the welterweight title several times; the movie star Robert Conrad; and the great pianist Roger Williams.

One day I walked up to the gym to work out and Gene Hackman was filming a movie about boxing. Many movies were made using Frankie's gym.

Joey and I would train several nights per week, plus Saturdays. Frankie refused to take money from me. So, I told him, I wouldn't come back unless I could take him to dinner twice a week, and he reluctantly agreed. I also gave him pro bono (free) legal advice. I used to spar with an FBI agent who was at my level of experience.

One night, as he was closing up, and I was banging the heavy bag, I heard him yelling at someone. There was a man in his twenties at the bottom of the stairs urinating. The man looked to me like the spitting image of Sonny Liston. Frankie: "What the fuck you doin'?" Man: "Pissin' on your stairs." Frankie: "I'm comin' down to whip your punk ass." The man ran away. He must have sensed that Frankie would destroy him.

I stayed close to Frankie for twenty years. I loved him very much. I told Joey that of all the people I knew, Frankie was one of the greatest. Decent, honest, and good, and the poor man couldn't make change for a nickel. I invited him to Joey's bar mitzvah and he was thrilled.

Frankie had a stroke about ten years ago and he couldn't speak anymore, except to say, "In the city." That is all he could say. He said it over and over. One of his daughters put him in a rest home in South Carolina (of all places), where she lived. I called Frankie every couple of months until he died last year. Although he couldn't speak, he managed to say, "I love you" to me. I will never forget this great man.

After Frankie's death, I started training at the famous Goosen Gym, where I became close friends with two brothers, seventeen and eighteen years old, who were just starting out as pros. I told them that they would both be world champions, and that is what they became. Rafael Ruelas, former lightweight champ, and Gabriel Ruelas, former superfeatherweight champ, are my very close friends after all these years.

Later, I began training at movie star Mickey Rourke's Outlaw Gym under the great trainer Freddie Roach. Freddie was Mickey Rourke's personal trainer. Freddie had fought for the featherweight title twice, once against Hector "Macho" Camacho and again against the great Bobby Chacon. Mickey Rourke was kind to me and did not even charge me. Several of my friends at the gym wanted me to fight him. They were convinced I'd beat him, but why fight a guy who was so nice to me?

One day I entered the gym and noticed that Mickey Rourke's face was caved in. Me: "What happened, Mick?" Mickey: "I was sparring with James Toney." James Toney is the former supermiddleweight champion of the world.

Freddie eventually bought him out and moved the gym, which is now located in Hollywood, under the name Wild Card Boxing Gym.

It is one of the most well-known boxing gyms in the country. Many movies are made there. Freddie Roach was recently named "Trainer of the Year" by *Ring Magazine*.

I train there regularly and at any given time, you will see former heavyweight champs, such as Michael Moorer and Franz Botha, lightweight champ Willy Jorrin, former lightweight champ Boom Boom Mancini, former featherweight champ Bobby Chacon, former supermiddleweight champ Frankie Liles, former supermiddleweight champ James Toney, who played Joe Frazier in the Ali movie, Robert Shapiro, Frank Stallone, and many other champions and celebrities.

I am happiest when I am with the boxers. I would rather be with one boxer than any hundred lawyers, and I tell them that. They are real. My trainers are Mac Foley, Pepper Roach, and Troy Boudoin, all former ranked pros. Each of them would step up to the plate for me in a minute, if I needed them.

Over the years, I am proud to say that I have helped many of them with minor criminal offenses such as drunk driving, fights, and other matters. They are very grateful and many of them would do anything for me. Frequently, when I enter the gym to work out, a number of the fighters say, "Here is Ken Green; he kept me out of the joint."

A few years before I retired from the public defender's office, I was in our lobby showing my head secretary some coffee stains near the elevator in the carpet that I wanted the janitor to clean. One of our bailout clients was screaming at the receptionist and threatening our attorneys. When I asked him to please keep the noise down, he attacked me, and I knocked him out.

If you ask a boxer a question, they will answer with one word. If you ask an attorney the same question, you will die of old age til they're through talking. A perfect example was a lawyer who I supervised when I was head deputy public defender. Let's call him John. One day I walked into court and watched John selecting a jury on a drunk driving case, known as a deuce. I noticed that several days later, he was still in the process of selecting the jury.

Me: "John, this is only a deuce case and the jury is looking bored." John: "You don't understand. I have to get into everything—the field sobriety tests, the chemical tests in detail, etc." Me: "O.K. John, but I'm telling you, they are very bored." Four days later. Me: "John, what's up with the case?" John: "We're just getting into some good cross-examination of the cop." Me: "John, let me be blunt. What's most important is that you not piss the jury off. You are pissing them off very much. Do you see juror Number 2, the blonde lady? She is thinking about her job and her kids. She doesn't give a rat's ass about your cross-examination and in fact could care less about the entire case. Check out juror Number 5, the man with the glasses. He's thinking about his mortgage and paying the bills and he has tuned you out a week ago. Wrap it up or your client is going in the toilet."

Six days later John is still trying the case. Me: "John, my man, you would be better off if you just shot your client in the head. He would have less pain than this jury will inflict on him all because you are full of yourself and putting your client second. This jury will put your client in the toilet five minutes after they go out to deliberate." John: "You'll see."

The jury deliberated seven minutes after hearing John's three-hour passionate closing argument, and like I predicted, John's client went straight into the toilet.

Why is it, I thought, that we don't have guys from Division Street trying these cases so the jury would dig them and if it's a close case they would give the call to the client?

Me a Teacher

I had just graduated from California State University in Los Angeles with a bachelor's degree in history. My parents were very proud. My first job out of college was with Allstate Insurance Company as a salesman. I lasted two months. My supervisor, an attorney turned insurance man, told me that I didn't know how to close a deal, and he was right. I just couldn't sell annuity policies to old people who didn't need them and who couldn't afford them.

I decided to go to law school at night, but I needed a day job because I had no money.

I decided that I would be a cop. The day that I was to take the entrance exam, I met Buddy Gold through an old Chicago friend.

Buddy was from Chicago and lived not far from my old neighborhood, but we had never met. He looked and sounded like Art Carney from the old Jackie Gleason show, "The Honeymooners." We bonded and Buddy told me that he taught junior high school in a very tough part of the county: a city called Hawaiian Gardens. He told me that his school needed teachers, and asked me if I wanted to take that job instead of being a cop. Me: "Buddy, I appreciate it, but I can barely speak English with my accent." Buddy: "The principal will love you. He needs tough guys."

Buddy and I drove down the next weekend and I met Murphy, who was the principal. He was a sweet Irish man with a twinkle in his eye.

Murphy: "You're just what I was looking for; a tough guy who the kids will love. Most of my teachers get walked all over, but that will not happen with you." The school was Killingsworth Junior High School. It was a small school with bungalow classrooms.

We got in his car and drove to the superintendent's office; she was in her office. She was a very nice lady and I was hired on the spot and signed a contract for $4,800 per year. I was thrilled to get it.

My first day on the job, I was very nervous. I was teaching seventh grade. I tried to speak like the one male teacher who I had in elementary school. It didn't work. Unless I spoke very slowly, there were too many "dees, dems, and dose." One day I told my best student, Betty, to "bring" something to the office. Betty: "Mr. Green, you mean take it to the office." Me: "Betty, I was just testing you!"

The kids liked me. After I'd been teaching one week, Murphy walked by my classroom. He looked through the window and did a double-take at the blackboard and motioned for me to come outside. Murphy: "Is that your printing on the blackboard?" Me: "Yeah, Murph." Murphy: "Why do you print?" Me: "My writing is illegible." Murphy: "You've gotta be kidding. Your printing is a shame to God. From now on, have one of the kids write on the board for you." He walked off with a smile on his face.

One day we had Open House. A mother approached Buddy Gold and asked, "Why is my son, Robert, getting failing grades?" Buddy: "Because he's dumb."

One of my students was Romeo Gaxiola. He was a young gangbanger. He terrorized all the kids who would then come and complain to me. After many warnings, I decided to put a stop to the terror.

One day after class, I told Romeo to remain. After all the kids left, I closed the door and shut the blinds. Me: "Romeo, sit down. I have employed various pedagogical tools for the purpose of intervention in order to ameliorate your aberrant behavior. I have been unsuccessful. Therefore, I have no alternative but to tell you, if you mess with any more kids ..." (and I left it hanging). Romeo: "No problem, Mr. Green." And there were no more problems."

About five years later, I was a public defender walking down the corridor of Juvenile Hall. I heard, "Mr. Green, Mr. Green." Without turning around, I recognized Romeo's voice, and said, "Romeo, I thought you'd be in the White House by now. Why are you here?" Romeo: "It was a frame-up, Mr. Green."

UCLA Professor

In 1976 I saw an ad in the *Los Angeles Daily Journal*. This is the legal newspaper for attorneys in L.A. There was an ad for an instructor to teach criminal law at UCLA Extension for the brand-new paralegal program. I applied and was hired. My good friend and an excellent trial lawyer, Deputy District Attorney Marsh Goldstein, put in a good word for me. Little did I know how much work was involved. I had to prepare the curriculum, prepare the quiz, the take-home assignments, and the final. I have been an adjunct professor in this program for twenty-seven years. Each year, I get the best evaluations of the twenty instructors.

Many of the comments state that I am real and I know how to convey the information. Thank you, Division Street.

Public Defender Rookie to Chief

When I was in my last semester of law school, I met Fred Manaster at a party.

Fred told me that he was a public defender, and the more he described his work, I thought that this job was made for me. Being Jewish, I had a natural leaning toward the underdog. I was liberal, then. Further, I grew up on the streets of Chicago, a rough area, and I was confident that the clients would respect me.

After I passed the bar, I called the department head, Richard Buckley, and asked if I could meet with him. To my surprise, he agreed. At our meeting, I told him that I wanted to be a criminal defense attorney. I could tell that he liked me. He told me to apply for the civil service exam. It was an oral interview conducted by the district attorney, the public defender, and county counsel. Each of them would make you an offer if they liked you.

When I arrived for the interview, I told the panel that I wasn't interested in anything but being a public defender. That's because I grew up with a lot of good people who took some wrong turns in life, like my barber Benny the Bookie and my street fighter pals.

The day after my interview, Mr. Buckley called and told me that I was hired, and it was one of the happiest days of my life. I knew within a week that this would be my life's work. I loved trials so much, I would have done it for nothing.

Fred, if I hadn't met you, who knows how my life would have turned out? Thank you, Freddy.

I had married before the bar results came out.

My father-in-law at the time I passed the bar was a very famous attorney who had as his partners the former governor of California, Goodwin Knight; the former attorney general, Evelle Younger; and Marcus Kaufman, retired California Supreme Court Justice, among others. The name of the firm was Buchalter, Nemer, Fields, and Savitch, and it was one of the most prestigious corporate and bankruptcy firms in Los Angeles. My father-in-law was Jerry Nemer. He was very disappointed that I rejected his offer to join the firm to become a low-life public defender.

But it was one of the wisest decisions I ever made, because I eventually divorced his daughter. More importantly, I just loved being a public defender.

Every day, for thirty years, I looked forward to going to work. And I eventually rose through the ranks to the position of bureau chief, where I supervised 360 attorneys and an additional 150 support staff.

I began my career with the Los Angeles County Public Defender's Office in January 1970. Among others in my class was Leslie Abramson. I also worked alongside Paul Fitzgerald, the lead attorney in the Charles Manson case. I worked alongside Jerry Chaleff, who represented one of the defendants in the Hillside Strangler case and became president of the Los Angeles Police Commission. There were many, many more public defenders that I worked with that went on to become rich and famous. That was because our office was the finest criminal defense firm in the world and still is.

My office was at the famous Hall of Justice, where Charles Manson's groupies (with bald heads and swastikas carved on their foreheads) would chant during his trial.

Being a public defender was fascinating. Every case was different and I enjoyed representing people whose liberty was on the line as opposed to representing businessmen who were suing each other for money.

As it was when I was a schoolteacher, I was very insecure about my heavy Chicago accent and my lack of exposure to culture. I came from a blue-collar neighborhood, where the words opera or tennis or literature would draw a blank stare. Division Street still haunted me.

The attorneys that I worked with in the public defender's office were, for the most part, in their first job right out of law school. Most were only about twenty-five years old, whereas I was thirty-two because I had to go to college and law school at night, and had interrupted my education with the military. Only a handful of them had been in the service. Most of them came from affluent families who put them through law school.

I set out an agenda for myself for the purpose of becoming the finest criminal defense attorney in Los Angeles. First, I would watch all the great attorneys in court, such as the flamboyant Gladys Towels Root, Charles Hollopeter, Harry Weiss (Sammy Weiss's uncle), Doug Dalton, Paul Caruso, and many others. I desperately wanted to sound like Perry Mason, eloquent and articulate, by trying to emulate others, but instead, I sounded like I came from the New York Bowery. I thought I stunk up the place. One of my supervisors, the late great Charlie English, told me to be myself, which was the best advice anyone had ever given me, because the juries loved me. Like Popeye said, "I am what I am." Later, when I trained lawyers, I passed this secret on to them.

I had been a public defender for three and a half years and loved it.

I was getting promoted quickly and had established an excellent reputation as a trial lawyer.

I had become friendly with another public defender whose father, Robert Pirosh, had won an Academy Award for writing the screenplay for *Battleground*, starring Aldo Ray.

Mike asked me if I wanted to leave the public defender's office and go into private practice with him. I declined and told him I loved being a public defender and wanted to make it my career. Finally, he went out on his own, but he kept calling me, telling me how much money he was making and that he bought a new Mercedes. My first wife also wanted me to have my own practice, and against my better judgment, I weakened and joined him.

Within one week, I knew that I had made one of the worst mistakes of my life, although we earned more money than I ever dreamed possible.

After six months, I bought a Mercedes and was rolling in money but I hated what I was doing. I hated it because I am compulsive and honest and could not go home until I returned each phone call. I could not charge for consultations. Usually, I was in my office until about midnight because, being a trial lawyer, I was in court all day. It was in the evening that I would interview new clients, prepare motions, and pay bills. We were so successful that we hired two secretaries, a paralegal, and a part-time attorney. However, we now had new problems, and that was the "nut." When we had problems with the help, Mike couldn't handle it, and I had to hire and fire and I didn't enjoy it.

One of the cases I had, I represented a man who was accused of breaking into the Hollywood Hills home of the widow of a recently deceased prominent civil rights attorney. The widow was coming home from church on a Sunday afternoon, and saw the defendant jumping out of her bedroom window and running through a meadow holding her jewelry. She ran to a neighbor's house, called the police, and they came within minutes and found the defendant running through the meadow with the jewelry. When I went to see the defendant in the jail, he asked me what I thought of the case, and I told him that I really liked it. He asked, "Do you know what really happened?" I told him yes. I told him that he was a good Samaritan, and that he was walking through the meadow, and saw a thief climbing out of a bedroom window, and decided to tackle him and retrieve the jewelry until the police came. He did so, but the thief ran away, and the police arrested him, thinking he was the burglar. He said, "How did you know?"

I represented another man who was charged with a serious crime, and during our discussion, he would constantly ask me what the level of my experience was. I tried to reassure him by telling him that I had been practicing law for eleven years when he looked at me in utter amazement and said, "That's the problem."

One of my clients was before the court for sentencing on an armed robbery. The judge, who was Jewish, turned to me and said, "Mr. Green, do you wish to be heard?" I said, *"Lozem gain"* (let him go).

My district attorney opponent was Lebanese. He said, "What does that mean?" Me: "It means, 'Have a nice day.'"

One day, I walked into the restroom in the Criminal Courts Building, and I saw a little black boy, and I said, "Hi, Junior," and his eyes got really wide. He said, "How do you know my name?" I said, "Not only do I know your name, I know how old you are." I took a guess and said six, and his eyes got wider and wider, and he said, "How do you know all that?" I told him I knew all about him. He ran out to the lobby and said, "Momma, Momma, there's a man who knows all about me."

On another occasion, I walked into the restroom in the Criminal Courts Building, and I saw a nude man washing his clothes in the washbasin. I asked him what he was doing, and he looked at me as if I was crazy and said he was washing his clothes.

I represented a Hispanic gentleman and when I tried to talk to him he kept saying, *"No comprendo Ingles."* I turned to him and said, *"Ret nisht ain vort"* (don't speak a word).

One of my favorite cases was a charge involving numerous federal bank robberies. I interviewed the defendant, and within minutes, I knew that he was crazy. For starters, whenever there's a federal case, and the feds defer to the states, you know that the defendant has mental problems, because in the federal courts, the burden is on the prosecution to prove that the defendant is sane, whereas in the state courts, the burden is on the defendant to prove that he is insane. So the feds simply didn't want any part of this case. I asked the defendant what he did with all the money that he stole from the banks, because they had him on videotape. With a straight face he told me that he was very fortunate because he used the money to buy porno films, and all he did all day was sit in his hotel room and whack off and then look at the bag of money and think, "What a fortunate fellow I am."

I once represented a man charged with multiple counts of rape. The prosecutor consolidated the trial, and about ten witnesses all testified that this was the man that raped them. He used the same m.o. After about the eighth woman testified, he leaned over to me and whispered, "Ask the woman if there was anything unusual about the rapist's dick." I asked him, "Why do you want me to do that?" He said, "Because I'm innocent, and I have warts on my dick. If I were the rapist, she would know that." He kept insisting, so finally, I asked. She said, "Actually yes, he had warts on it."

When I first began working as a public defender, our office represented a white lady who was charged with shoplifting. She was assigned a Hispanic public defender. She went to our supervisor and said, "I don't want any spics, any niggers, or any chinks or Kikes." My supervisor, who had a great sense of humor, called over a man named Carlos, who spoke impeccable English. He asked Carlos, "Carlos, have you learned any English yet?" Carlos said, "*Poquito.*" The supervisor told the woman, "This is your attorney." Carlos is now a judge.

I was selecting a jury one day and asked a juror if he had ever been the victim of a crime, and he said "Yes, every April 15."

When I was a rookie public defender, my partner and I were in a court before one of the toughest judges. He was a former West Pointer. Everyone was terrified of him. He was particularly fond of my partner. When the judge would take the bench in the morning, he would look at my partner and say, "Good morning, Mike." Mike would smile and say, "Good morning, your Honor," and under his breath, but loud enough for me to hear, he'd say, "You no-good motherfucker."

I worked for one of the most infamous judges, Noel Cannon, who was ultimately thrown off the bench. Her chambers were painted pink, and she held a dog on her lap during court. All of the attorneys were terrified of her. She would constantly put public defenders in the lockup if they annoyed her. One day she got pulled over for a traffic ticket outside the courthouse and she told the cop, "If you give me a ticket, I'll give you a .38 vasectomy." She was ultimately thrown off the bench.

Next door to her was Judge Leland Geiler. He was also thrown off the bench. During my first week as a public defender, I walked into his court and I saw him running around the court during recess with a dildo, terrifying the court reporter and the clerk, and he chased one of the public defenders as well.

Shortly after Mike and I went into private practice, I was appointed on a high-publicity case along with cocounsel Charles Lloyd, who was one of the most prominent black attorneys in Los Angeles. Charles had been the partner of Mayor Tom Bradley some years back.

Our clients were charged with ninety-nine counts of robbery, burglary, and rape. They had allegedly walked into a high-stakes poker game room and had all of the players strip naked and put all their jewelry and money in pillowcases. Additionally, they were alleged to have raped three of the women players. The police were called by some of the neighbors who had seen them walk up the stairs. When the police arrived, they ordered them by bullhorn to come downstairs with their hands up. When they didn't comply, the police charged the apartment, and found twenty naked people, and three men who were partially unclothed who had guns at their feet. The cops said, "Who are the crooks?" And everyone pointed to the three men who would become our clients. We went to trial and the jury returned a verdict of guilty on all ninety-nine counts and the defendants were looking at about fifty years in prison each. The judge asked if we wanted to poll the jury, and I said yes. The last juror, a black woman, told the judge that this was not her verdict, and that the white jurors coerced her. The judge, rather than send the jury back to deliberate, engaged them in a dialogue, and as a result, I made a motion for a mistrial on the grounds that this juror was totally intimidated and our clients could not get a fair trial. The judge agreed. The case was retried a month later; we received not-guilty verdicts on all ninety-nine counts. I was told that this was a record for not-guilty verdicts.

Charles Lloyd was an outstanding attorney, and he was also an ordained reverend. He spoke about religion and slavery and he had all the jurors crying. When he passed near me during his eloquent argument, I whispered, "Charlie, enough already, you're going to make me cry too." Charlie is still a dear friend of mine.

I was a rookie and was assigned a case where my client was charged under a bestiality statute (100 years old) with having unlawful sexual intercourse with a fowl. I walked into the lockup at the defendant's arraignment and there were about ten other men in the cell. Client: "What's the beef?" Me: "It's not quite beef. It is fowl." Client: "What am I charged with?" Me: "Sir, you are charged with unlawful sexual intercourse with a fowl." Client: "Say what?" Me: "You're charged with fuckin' a chicken." Client: "Thanks."

On another occasion, I had a client who was a rookie robber and had gone into a liquor store and pointed his gun at the bartender and the customers and said, "O.K., you mother stickers, this is a fuckup."

Many of my clients would find God for the first time after committing some horrendous crime. They would walk into court holding the Bible. I would tell them that in Department 117, I was God. For example, Willie had broken into a woman's house and sodomized her. He then cut off her breasts. Willie always carried a Bible.

Another client was Wilma, an African-American woman. She decided to punish her two little grandsons because they would cry for food. Wilma put them in scalding hot water in the bathtub with a bluing chemical, which bleached their skin. Wilma always carried a Bible.

The stories go on and on, and each day I looked forward to hearing the next one. I used to walk down the hall to kibitz with my friend Ned Cook. He worked in an office off a hallway known as asshole alley because it led to the men's room. This was the type of humor we developed in order to be able to handle the strain of our jobs.

We had been in practice sixteen months when Mike's twenty-nine-year-old wife (a lovely girl) was diagnosed with bone marrow cancer, and she died very quickly.

Unfortunately, at this point in my life, my marriage was failing. I thought I would die of the pain to leave my baby son and suffer a divorce, but it happened.

At the end of one workday, Mike came into my office and poured us each a drink.

Me: "Mike, I want to go back to the public defender's office." Mike: "Me too." And so we did.

We turned over our pending cases to an attorney I'll call Joe who I had met when I was studying for the bar. I thought he was honest, but boy was I wrong. We drew up a fee arrangement for the many, many cases that we still had. For several months, this attorney abided by it.

One day, while Mike and I were back in our public defender offices, I heard Mike say, "Why, why?" Me: "Mike, what is wrong?" Mike: "Joe decided to dishonor our fee agreement and told me he will give us no more money even though he still has many, many cases left that would amount to thousands of dollars that we are due." I got on the phone and persuaded Joe that this was wrong. He reconsidered and paid us for a while, but then reneged again. We finally had to hire Paul Fitzgerald, who had been the lead attorney on the Charles Manson case, and he got us a good settlement.

Mike and I had returned to the public defender's office, but we lost our rank.

We had left the office as grade threes but had to return as grade ones; that was a huge cut in pay. The rule was, if you're gone more than one year you must start all over again. After one more year, Mike left again because there were no promotions or pay raises.

Mike became a judge a few years later; he got connected with a powerful fundraiser named Sheldon Andelson, who had the ear of the governor.

After ten years as a trial attorney, I was promoted to head deputy, where I was in charge of two separate courthouses. About three years later, I was promoted again to division chief, and two years after that to bureau chief, where I was the third-highest-ranking administrator in the office. It was a wonderful career, and I retired two years ago, having served thirty years.

In my old neighborhood of Division Street, we had an expression: "I need an angel." That is someone who goes out of their way to help you with your life.

Bill Littlefield was my angel in the public defender's office. He was the head of the department and a legend. A man's man, a war hero, and the most decent man I ever knew, like Frankie Goodman. He believed in me and trusted me. He promoted me four times until I became bureau chief. What a thrill—I was a senior partner in the finest and largest criminal law firm in the world.

Bill, at age nineteen, volunteered to fight behind enemy lines at Luzan and Leyte in World War II as an officer in the Alamo Scouts—the forerunner of the Rangers. After the war, he became a public defender when it wasn't the popular thing to do. He served for thirty-six years, eighteen years as the department head. He is now eighty years old and has been retired since 1993; he is one of my best friends. I see him all the time. My wife and son and I revere him. I hope he lives forever.

Returning to My Roots

On one of our visits, I decided that I must go back to my grammar school, Von Humboldt. I had a fantasy of sitting behind my desk with the built-in inkwell in my seventh grade class. I hadn't been in that school since I graduated in 1951 (more than half a century ago). I called the school and asked for the principal. He was a dees, dems, and dose guy; looked about in his late sixties; and was very friendly, a prince of a man. I told him that I was an attorney from Los Angeles and graduated from his school many years ago and may I visit?

Principal: "Do you remember where the school is?" Me: "Of course." Principal: "It's bad here. Pull up to the main door, get out, and don't look back. Come in quick. We have a guard."

I walked into the school with my wife Maureen and my good friend Gerry Zaidman, video camera at the ready. Immediately upon entering, I started to cry. Everything looked the same. The inside of the school was immaculate, the floors were polished with a high gloss, but the exterior looked like a war zone with bullet holes in the building and a police barricade in the front from a recent shooting.

We walked into the principal's office, which I had remembered as being huge, but it was the size of a closet. We sat down elbow to elbow, and the window was open, and there were ugly huge crows on the ledge making crow noises.

Principal: "What year did you graduate?" Me: "Fifty-one." He got up from his chair and went into what looked like a closet. I guess it was the archives. He returned in less than thirty seconds, and he handed me an old school newspaper, and said, "Is this you?" My photo and Gerry's photo were in it. We both had tears in our eyes.

Principal: "Would you guys like to speak to some classes?" Gerry and me: "Sure." The vice principal escorted us. The kids were all children of color—approximately 75% Puerto Rican and 25% black. There were no whites at all. When I went to the school, it was 40% Jewish, approximately 30% Polish, and the remaining 30% were the children of immigrants of other European countries.

The vice principal introduced us and told the kids that we had attended this school a long time ago, and that we had lived across the street.

I pointed out the window to where my apartment building had been, which had long since been razed.

Before I could begin speaking, one of the girls said, "Was it as bad then as it is now?" Me: "We were all poor, but Gerry and I made it." Girl: "What does 'make it' mean?" We had the privilege of speaking to many more classes and hopefully we inspired some of the kids. It was an extremely moving experience. I hated to leave the principal. I wanted to take him home.

We got back in the car, and had driven only about two blocks when we saw a number of young black men hanging out on a wooden porch. Suddenly, one of them ran right in front of Gerry's Lincoln, and made a gang sign. I reached for my gun, which I always carry in California, but of course, the gun wasn't there because I'm not licensed in Illinois.

Me: "Gerry, do you have what it takes to run this motherfucker down?" Gerry: "Of course." Gerry stepped on the pedal and the hoodlum backed off and we got out of there. This incident is on videotape.

A few years ago, I was in Chicago on one of my annual visits. My oldest friends and I were driving around the old neighborhood (what we call the swoop). Ahead of us, a cop was directing traffic; a funeral was passing. My friend Earl didn't stop fast enough and the cop banged his fist on his hood and said, "You stupid motherfucker, stop when I tell youse." Me: "God, it's good to be home."

For the past ten consecutive years, my wife Maureen and I have visited Chicago. The first night of our trip is spent visiting with my friends at the great steak house, Myron & Phil's, in Skokie. All the boys show up with their wives and we reminisce and celebrate our success. The wives express their gratitude that we didn't go to prison or end up working at the corner gas station changing tires.

The next day, the boys pick me up in an S.U.V. and we spend the day "swooping." We begin by driving through Division Street from one end to the other, and we ride through Humboldt Park. We drive by Von Humboldt Grammar School and each of the boys' old apartment buildings as well as all the places we used to hang out. The neighborhoods are extremely dangerous but we keep doing it. Last year, we drove by Starkman's old apartment. He stopped the car, got out, went into the vestibule, touched his old mailbox, and cried, while I looked out for gangbangers.

The next day, I repeat the whole thing alone in my rental car. I guess a shrink would have a good time analyzing why I am compelled to do this year after year after year. Is it because I am grateful that I escaped my perceived destiny of working at the corner gas station? Or is it because I have good memories of my childhood? I don't know. I do know that Division Street keeps drawing me back. I cannot stay away.

A few years ago, I was reading the *Los Angeles Daily Journal*. This is a legal newspaper read by attorneys in Los Angeles. Every day they profile a judge or a well-known attorney. On this particular day, they profiled the president of the San Francisco Bar Association. I immediately recognized the name and the photograph. In the first sentence of the article, he stated that he grew up on Division Street in Chicago. I called Mel and he remembered me. We played basketball together at Saint Fidelis basketball court. I told him that I was proud of him because he didn't forget where he came from.

Retirement The Golden Years and a Look Back

When you work for the government, you are like a soldier. I had to be at my desk at 7:30 a.m., even though my position was chief. I refused to bend the rules for myself when I would not do so for the 360 lawyers that I supervised.

For the thirty years that I worked for the government, I was out of bed at 5 a.m. to go running and do my sit-ups, shadow box, jump rope, pump weights, and then go to work.

I tried over 100 jury trials and rarely gave a closing argument that exceeded fifteen minutes and I won an awful lot of cases.

Many of the jury trials that I tried, I did in one day from start to finish. I won because the jurors thought the case could not be too important if it was that fast and they liked me because I didn't bore them with bullshit.

Example: I was one of six cocounsels on a six-defendant fraud trial. Of course, I had the heavy; the public defender always takes the heavy because we are the best lawyers and the heavy needs the best lawyer. I was cross-examining a prosecution witness and when I finished, the judge called all the attorneys to the bench and said, "Ken, you didn't clear any of the testimony up and the jury is totally confused." Me: "Judge, thank you very much, but if I cleared it up, my client goes directly into the toilet."

Whenever I announced ready for trial, the judge would ask for a time estimate. The DA would frequently say six or seven days, and I would always say one day. The judge would say, "Why the variance?" Me: "Your honor, I cannot understand why it takes more than one day for the jurors to learn the truth about the case."

I tried lots of cases against Deputy D.A. Tom Herman, who is now a judge and a great guy. I kept beating him over and over again.

One day, he said, "It just occurred to me what you have been doing. You have been doing a tap dance on my bald head by picking all women on your juries and they have a crush on you."

I tried a case against a deputy D.A. who I will call Jim. He was the most boring D.A. in history. The poor guy must have taken too many left hooks because he was exceptionally dull-witted and boring. On voir dire (a Latin term for jury selection, meaning to speak the truth), he asked a little old lady if she had ever been accused of the same crime that the defendant was accused of. The defendant was charged with robbery. He asked another prospective juror, a female, about twenty-five years old, if she had any children. When she said yes, he said, "Are they grown and out of the house?" I then knew I owned this jury.

He was personally arrogant to me. His closing argument exceeded two hours and then it was my turn. Me: "Oooo-eee. Did he bore you like he bored me?" They were hysterical. Me: "He said nothing, no evidence, no proof, no nothing, just words, like heretofore, and subsequent. I will now speak for five minutes. Watch the time, and if I exceed five minutes raise your hand and I will stop in mid-sentence. Show him what you think of his argument and go in that deliberation room and do the right thing." I got a ten-minute not-guilty verdict.

Twice a week, I go in the ring and spar or work the mitts. I then bang the heavy bag, use the speed bag and the slip bag, and jump rope and shadow box. I have also been appointed to the board of directors of a Los Angeles Police Department boxing club for at-risk children. The coach is my longtime friend, Byron Martinez. Almost every day, for about an hour, I help the kids with their boxing skills and talk to them about the importance of an education, and I tell them about how I became a lawyer having come from Division Street. The great former welterweight champion of the world, Carlos Palomino, volunteers his time there, and he is a great role model because not only was he a great fighter, but he is a college graduate. The kids who go there are almost all Mexican, and they all call me by my first name and we are very friendly. When I arrive, we all touch knuckles, which is the greeting among fighters. I bonded with one kid in particular, an eleven-year-old named Jesus Rodriguez, who is known by the name "Tank" because he has no fear in the ring and keeps coming. I told him that I believe he will be world champion someday, because he is such a good fighter. When the timing is right, I always ask him how he is doing in school. Recently, I was walking out of the gym heading toward my car and he followed me. He said, "Ken, I got a C+ on my math test yesterday, and I got a B on my English test." I told him that I grew up like he did and that I became a lawyer, and that I want to see him achieve the greatness that I know is within him. When I got in my car, it made me cry. Recently, a gang member shot him in the foot as he was walking home. He had done nothing, except be in the wrong place at the wrong time. I am working with the police, and we will catch the shooter, and he will pay. Oh yes, he will pay.

Dino—Down for the Count

Forty years have passed since my best friend and I went our separate ways. We were like brothers since kindergarten, to the age of twenty-four, when I left Chicago for L.A.

Our parents were best friends and my mother kept me up to date on Dino's life. He was institutionalized at age twenty-five—a mental institution paid for by the V.A. He had been a soldier all of three months and that earned him V.A. benefits. During that forty-year interval, I saw him only once.

I came to Chicago for a visit at age forty-five and called his mother.

Me: "Ruth, it's Kenny Green. I'm in town. Can I see Donny?" Ruth: "He lives in a mental institution but he will be visiting with us this weekend so come over on Saturday."

I walked up the winding creaky stairs to their tiny co-op apartment. Dino was in the living room and looked very old. His mother and father were there, too. I hugged him and he said, "You look very strong. I want to tell you something so come in the bedroom." He closed the door. "I slept with Judy Reynolds, who went all through grammar school with us and was so beautiful. Also, I want you to know that I am financially set for life. I never have to work again. I get $800 per month S.S.I." The conversation went downhill from there.

The next night, my aunt made a party for Dino's parents and me; Ruth and Max attended, along with some other friends and family.

Ruth was always very quiet except when she used to call Dino and me bums when she thought we didn't study in college. She would say, "Bums are what you are and you will never amount to anything because you don't shtudy."

That night at my aunt's party, Ruth motioned for me to come into an empty room. Ruth (crying hysterically): "Kenny, you were his best friend. What happened to my Donny?" Me: "Ruth, I wish I knew. I would give anything to know. At age sixteen, all of the boys noticed that he started acting goofy after he broke up with Adrienne but we thought it was all an act."

According to his sister Linda, the shrinks gave him many labels but were unable to cure him.

On one of my last visits to Chicago, I had lunch with Linda. Me: "Linda, tell me all you can about his mental illness." Linda: "He has been institutionalized for almost forty years and no one has come to visit him except for me and my parents, who are now both dead. The shrinks gave him many labels but really didn't know what was wrong with him, but two years ago one of the women shrinks told me that she could cure him. I laughed and said good luck. After six months, the shrink said, 'It's hopeless.'"

When I started my yearly pilgrimage to Division Street ten years ago, I found out which facility Dino was at but Linda told me not to go. She said he probably wouldn't want to see me and also that his brain is fried from all the medication and he talks to himself.

Starting about seven years ago, on each of my trips to Chicago, I would drive my rental car to the institution—sometimes with my wife Maureen, and sometimes with some of the boys. A few times, I would walk up to the door, but couldn't bring myself to go in. A few times I would actually walk into the lobby and turn around and leave. I did this for seven years.

Finally, last December, I decided I needed closure; I drove to the facility all by myself in a rental car. It was cold and rainy and I parked in front. It was a very bad neighborhood.

The people who were gathered in front were either in wheelchairs or using walkers and all of them looked like homeless people. Ninety-nine percent were people of color, black, Mexican, or Puerto Rican.

I wanted to see his face without talking to him. I didn't want to upset him, so I wore a hat and shades in the hope that he wouldn't recognize me. I just wanted to look at him and leave.

I didn't want to stop at the front desk, believing that they wouldn't allow me in. I carried a clipboard and pretended I knew where I was going. The stench of urine was overpowering. All the people were mumbling to themselves. At the front desk were about eight Filipino nurses. I walked right past them. There were about thirty rooms on the lobby floor, and the place was absolutely filthy. There were nameplates on each door and I walked from room to room, reading "Garcia, Washington, Gonzales." I went to all thirty rooms. Finally, I saw a Filipino nurse and casually said, "Where's Solomon?" Nurse: "Solomon?" Me: "Yes." Nurse. "Oh, you mean Don Solomon. He's on the fourth floor." I hunted for the elevator and got on and pressed the button for the fourth floor. There were four pathetic people on the elevator, all raggedy, unkempt, and talking to themselves. I got off on the fourth floor and began to hyperventilate. Every nameplate had either a black or Hispanic name like "Willy Washington," "Guadalupe Garcia," etc. I went from room to room and finally I got to the very last room in the corner, at the end of the hall, and saw the name "Don Solomon" on the nameplate.

I entered the room and began to sweat profusely. There were five cots in a shabby, cold room. There were two white men in the room. One was sitting up on his cot watching a tiny TV and was oblivious to me. He seemed wasted. At the end of the room was Dino lying on his back sleeping, hooked up to an oxygen machine. Linda had told me that he had emphysema from fifty years of smoking. He was asleep and this once-handsome young man who was a great athlete now weighed no more than 130 pounds and was totally bald. In high school he weighed 200 pounds, solid muscle. I stood over him, tears falling down my cheeks. I walked out and I knew that I would never see him again.

It's Just You and Me, Daddy

My son Joey was a gift from God. I had to leave his mother when he was only six months old. It was constructive termination. Without going into details, for me to leave this beautiful child, my life must have been hell and it was.

From the day his mother and I separated, I was never a weekend father.

I would pick him up every day after work and wheel him around in his buggy. We were always together. The movie *Kramer vs. Kramer* was our story. I was Dustin Hoffman's age and Joey was the same age as his son.

I tried to get custody of him starting at age two but every time we walked into court, my ex had her father and one of the senior partners along with her. The judge took one look at my powerful and famous attorney father-in-law and it was all over.

I tried several times and even though I was prepared to make an extremely strong case that I was the more fit parent and that it would be in my son's best interest to be with me, I had no chance.

Finally, when Joey turned seven, his mother asked me if I wanted custody on a "trial basis." She told me if I didn't take him she would put him in a boy's home. I was thrilled at the thought of getting him, but knew if I let on, to spite me, she would withdraw the offer. I knew the "trial basis" meant she'd never want him back.

I drew up the court order, had her sign it, and walked it through the court the next day and had the judge sign it on the spot. Ordinarily this process takes months.

The first night I brought Joey home, I tucked him in bed and he looked up at me and said, "Well, Daddy, I guess it's just you and me from now on."

How his mother could give up this sweet, beautiful boy will forever astound me. Every day I was with him, I thanked God. His mother, never once in the eighteen years he lived with me, ever called to see how he was.

I was his mother, father, and best friend. We would get up at 5:30 a.m. during the week and go to the gym. I would then drop him off at a deserted school two hours before class started so I could get to work downtown at 8 a.m. Sometimes it was still dark out when I dropped him off. I had an arrangement with the only person who was there that early—a cafeteria worker who would watch him while he sat nearby doing his homework. At 3 p.m. a bus would pick him up and take him to the Jewish day care center, where I would pick him up at 6 p.m. if I got there on time. If traffic was heavy, the counselor would take him to his or her house and I'd pick him up there. We then went out to dinner because there was no time to cook. I then helped him with his homework and I allowed him to watch one hour of TV, and then bedtime at 8:30 p.m.

I packed his lunch and always put a note in the bag that said, "Daddy loves you."

I used to mail him letters telling how honored I am to be his father. He would open the mailbox and read them.

When we came home from dinner and I parked the car in the carport, he'd always ask me to measure him against the mark I made the night before on the carport post to see if he grew. I lived for these moments and his constant questions: "Daddy, why do people grow? How do planes fly?"

He never complained. Thanks to you, Joey, for all your sacrifices. I did my best. He is now a public school teacher in special education and has two master's degrees and will soon begin work on his PhD. He is married to a wonderful girl named Christina, who is also a schoolteacher with a master's degree.

He calls me every day to tell me he loves me.

Maureen

When I was a teenager, my father gave me great advice. Dad: "Boychik, when you pick a girl to marry, make sure that she loves her mother." Boy, was my old man smart.

Maureen adores her mother and that warms my heart.

We met fourteen years ago; she was my student at UCLA. She decided to take the year-long paralegal course to help her decide if she should go to law school.

At the conclusion of the course, she called me to arrange for her to sit in on the Night Stalker case. I asked her out to lunch during the trial, and the rest is history.

Maureen went back to Northern California where her family lived. She enrolled in Santa Clara Law School and we had a long-distance relationship for four years.

I didn't fly, so I took the train one weekend and she would fly in to L.A. the next weekend.

We've been married for nine years. Boy, did I get lucky. Maureen is 100% devoted to me and me to her. She is solid gold. She is a deputy district attorney in Los Angeles.

What is there about Division Street that motivated me and so many others to reach our highest potential? Was it our loving parents? Was it the strong bonding we had with our friends? Was it the role models who preceded us?

Or was there indeed some magic on Division Street?

This is my journey from Division Street. I'm getting ready to go back next month.

When I decided to write this book, I told my wife that I will do it Division Street style. No extra words, just tell my story, and that's what I have tried to do.